Imagination

Introduction
Stephen Bayley

The right words, according to Lenin, are worth a hundred regiments. So the right words and pictures carry even more firepower in the international battle for the consumer's attention. Factor in architecture and lighting, music and theatre and you can forget local territorial squabbles: you may have won the entire world war.

Lenin was speaking when commercial truths and practices were as straightforward and unambiguous as moral ones. When the Russian Revolution was news, advertising depended on simple claims, not elaborate imagery, still less 'brand experiences' occurring in architectural space. And there was only one medium, print. Two, if you count posters. In 1917, design, too, was a simple proposition. It was still ten years before a handful of slick New Yorkers – with backgrounds in window-dressing and the stage and foregrounds full of sharp tailoring, dentistry and chutzpa – would create the consultant design profession and style America's fatigued consumers out of recession. No, in 1917 design, if it was known at all, was still an extension of craft sensibility: unworldly dreamers in the Cotswolds, nurturing fantasies about medieval life in the country.

The twenty-first century is different. We are not, it is said, going to die of ignorance. We are going to die of complexity. The excess is baffling. Never before in the history of industrialized capitalism has there been so much choice, confusion, segmentation, media fragmentation, data smog and popular bewilderment. The British market alone sustains more than one hundred magazines devoted to motor vehicles. There is over-supply and under-demand: there are some product categories where the consumer's desire has shrunk to a level where only the most sensitive instruments can detect it.

This was the prevailing condition of the US market in 1927, when Raymond Loewy, Norman Bel Geddes, Henry Dreyfuss and others invented styling. In Detroit, Harley Earl did exactly the same for General Motors. While from the moment Henry launched his sputtering gasoline buggy down a Michigan dirt track, Ford had dominated the US auto market, by the mid-20s everyone who needed a car had bought a Model-T. It was left to a different type of entrepreneur to realize that making these cars look interesting may have some commercial potential. That entrepreneur was Harley Earl.

The design revolution that followed was more cheerful than the Russian one that preceded it, but it was a victory so complete that no more battles need to be fought. Everyone still in business knows that their products have to give the customer what Earl called a 'visual receipt' for his cash. Today we have a similar revolution in perceptions and practices. So the design business has moved on. It is not concerned with simply re-shaping products, but with re-shaping entire sensibilities. It operates not in simple national markets where industry and retail are neatly integrated vertically, but in a global miasma of brand awareness. What is a brand? It is the mixture of associations and expectations that all successful products possess.

It is in this more nuanced culture that Imagination has become Britain's, and by some measures the world's, biggest design agency. We don't use the word 'consultancy' anymore on account of inappropriate quaintness. The range of Imagination's work stretches conventional definitions of design. Yes, of course, they have someone who could streamline a wastepaper basket for you; they probably even have someone who could engineer an ergonomic backrest. They have people who, if anyone actually cared any more, could probably foment outrage at the Milan Furniture Fair. But Imagination marches to a different beat. It flourishes in a world where the appearance of individual products or specific environments is no longer the solitary end and aim of 'design'. Does Imagination have a 'style'? No, not really. Does Imagination have an 'offer'? You bet!

The facts are convincing. In 1968, Gary Withers, a St Martin's School of Art graduate with a modest job as a trade show stand designer for the DuPont chemical company, was sitting in a pub. A chance contact led to some moonlighting. Soon Withers was at a long-forgotten firm called Gerald Green Associates. A move to Saffron Hill in Holborn gave rise to Saffron Design Associates. By 1978 this had become Imagination and there was a staff of fifteen. Now it is nearer five hundred. Turnover in 1984, when bigger premises were found in Covent Garden's Bedford Street, was £8 million. Now it is more than £130 million. Imagination's landmark premises in Store Street are already 9,300 sq m (100,000 sq ft), but there's a plan afoot to build Imagination City, a truly large-scale living, working creative community, either on a greenfield site or in a regenerated inner city location.

In business terms, the extraordinary growth has been almost entirely organic, which is to say that for twenty years, Imagination has been consistently (and, as it happens, uniquely) offering its corporate customers a fully integrated range of services for which there is – evidently – so much demand that the agency has grown to a size more usually associated with advertising

than design companies. This is because Imagination is stretching the definition of what 'design' means. It is true that an architectural practice called Herron Associates was acquired in 1989, whose principal, the late Ron Herron, was a member of the influential Archigram group and therefore a profound influence on Richard Rogers and Norman Foster. Interior designers, Virgile & Stone, became a subsidiary company a year later, but in all essentials Imagination has built itself. A New York office opened in 1988, a Detroit one in 1999 and a Hong Kong one in 2000. The Michigan office services Ford, Imagination's longest-standing client, while the Asian presence is a statutory requirement of doing business in China. That Ford intends to become the world's leading consumer products company and that China represents the largest pool of unexploited consumer potential on the planet is eloquent enough of Imagination's own ambitions.

What makes Imagination so different and so successful? Gary Withers sees himself as a team player and, unusually for someone knee-deep in the media business, does not seek personal publicity, but it is nonetheless true that Imagination's personality has been shaped by his own. It would be ludicrous to suggest that Withers is an unworldly, self-effacing recluse, but his philosophy and personal style are a world away from those other figures who in their time built influential design businesses. Historically, these other designer-entrepreneurs led, to return to a military analogy, from the front. The Imagination organization is much flatter. One for all and all for one.

Raymond Loewy was a flamboyant, photogenic, pomaded hustler who scuffed the frontier between kitsch and genius, splashing chrome and ego wherever he went. Even Charles Eames, perhaps the most cerebral designer of them all, allowed his personality to dominate perceptions of his work. Eliot Noyes, the man who gave us IBM as 'Big Blue', a Himalayan peak in the history of corporate identity, never built a huge business: his achievements for IBM and Mobil were based on close personal relationships with the company Chairmen. In our own time, by contrast, Terence Conran's design ethic was inspired by a sort of indulgent aesthetic hedonism, fruit of a weird marriage between Walter Gropius and Elizabeth David. Conran taught the world to take pleasure either in an interior design version of Escoffier's imprecation *Faites simple,* or in Bauhaus restraint. Splendid, but different. Gary Withers acknowledges the Bauhaus too, but not only in terms of style. For

Withers, the achievement of the Bauhaus was not about right angles or industrial materials, but in successfully harmonizing an eclectic bunch of talented individuals into a coherent group mentality. Imagination is the expression of a showman-impresario rather than a world-improver. When an event for a client required the windows to be taken out of Versailles, Imagination took the windows out of Versailles. It seems straightforward, but no-one had thought of it before.

What Withers has done with Imagination is to take design to the next level. Until Imagination, no design consultancy was able to rival advertising agencies in terms of cool professionalism. The older consultancies may have been able to offer style, taste, occasional hysteria, philosophy, but too often they were working against the client's ambitions. That, after all, is what world-improving design is all about. Why be a designer unless you want to change things? Imagination is different, preferring to project and enhance existing sensibilities rather than radically reconsider them.

A strength of Imagination from the very start has been its close links with advertising agencies. So often in the past, older design consultancies were hobbled and frustrated by agencies who, holding the majority of a client's available funds, did a lot of poo-poohing about alternative initiatives which might require a budget of their own. Never mind that agencies had neither the skill nor the inclination to design graphics or interiors, and certainly had no idea about how to make money out of them. It is in this last area that the basis of Imagination's unique business performance lies. The job arising from that chance encounter in a pub led to Withers being involved in a pitch to a major tobacco company, not as a jobbing itinerant showroom designer, but actually as a part of the agency team. Withers soon found himself belonging to an agency, a relationship that ended with a management buy-out that started the Imagination story. From the beginning, Imagination has looked at the total business picture, and in doing so has been able to charge fees that reflect this breadth. Of course, it is difficult to say whether Imagination's impressive growth is a by-product of, or the reason for, the recent structural change in the character of design. We live in an age characterized by French sociologist Jean Baudrillard as enjoying (if that's the right word) an 'ecstasy of communication'. Design is everywhere: it is even on television. There is, perhaps, nowadays less of a case for 'consultant' design when every financially solvent company employs its own.

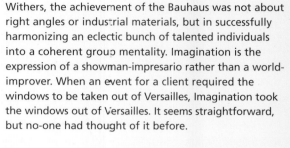

Facing page, the Imagination Building on Store Street, London, home to Imagination and Virgile & Stone. Right, the offices of Imagination Global Investor Communications on Bedford Street, London. A second office opened in Hong Kong in 2000. Far right, the New York City office of Imagination USA Inc. The company also has an office in Detroit, Michigan.

Instead, what Withers has done is apply his St Martin's design education not to the execution of objects in fastidious Museum-of-Modern-Art-endorsed style, but to the conception, organization and implementation of roadshows, exhibitions, conferences, events and a wide range of experiential communications projects. That this has exactly matched industry's need for 'brand experiences', roadshows and a general and continuing enlargement of appetite for exhibitions and events of all sorts may be simply good luck. But as Andre Agassi once remarked, 'The more I practise, the luckier I get'. Imagination has consistently practiced in a field whose borders it defined and enlarged. In terms of credibility and achievement, it stands almost alone in that same field.

The turning point was in the early 80s when automotive presentations, including product launches and motor shows, were a significant part of Imagination's business. A successful exhibition stand requires all the disciplines that Imagination either possessed or needed to acquire: running temporary projects to a scary timetable, designing installations with an arresting profile, access to engineering skills, creating strong graphics, but all the time being mindful of public access and the client's expectations. A motor show is high-octane theatre with a degree in typography and a genius for lighting thrown in. By the time you have done one or two, you also know about materials, crowd management, data capture and logistics.

At one point Imagination had contracts with no less than eleven automotive manufacturers, but after agreeing to drop Mazda, Fiat, British Leyland, Citroën, Berliet and the rest, Ford was prepared to make a long-term commitment to Imagination against a promise of exclusivity. For Ford this arrangement had the benefit of simplifying and consolidating its face-to-face communications activity (where hitherto there had been an expensive form of *ad hocism* with a roster of designers, shopfitters and various other contractors). For Imagination, the arrangement had the benefit of a privileged association with a vast company with international credentials and a communications programme on a scale to match.

Again, whether it is symptom or cause is tricky to determine, but within two decades, motor shows had evolved from boozy garage-culture events where the chief concession to cultural interest was a girl in a sequinned bikini with a panache in her back-combed

hair, to being theatres of brand values. This close relationship with Ford, which has encompassed retail schemes and strategic consultancy as well as exhibitions and presentations, also coincided with the car company's own decision to evolve from being a reliable, but mundane, Anglo-American provider of blue-collar cars to becoming a design-led world-class manufacturer with a boggling portfolio of products.

It began with the launch of the Ford Cargo truck, for which Imagination virtually reconstructed a lake-side conference centre in Montreux. Shortly after, with a staff of less than twenty, Imagination launched the then audacious Sierra in 1982, with events taking place in Docklands and the Palais des Congrès in Paris. This was in fourteen languages, so they learnt a bit about diplomacy in the process too. The trade launch of the Orion at Castle Ashby in Northamptonshire soon followed. They say you had to be there. The fastidious might mutter smoke and mirrors, but everyone who saw it remembers with astonishment the after-dinner effect of a solid stately home melting away into the presentation of an Escort with a boot. It was a brash theatrical concept, made possible by a bit of nerve and even more heavy mechanical plant. British Telecom soon followed (and remained) as a major corporate client. Just about the first thing Imagination did for the pioneering TelCo was build a geodesic dome weighing nine tons and astonish people with it at the National Exhibition Centre. Like the windows being taken out of Versailles, it was just a case of daring to imagine. Every case history of Imagination and its relationships with its clients consistently shows how astonished people have been and that, astonishment, a by-product of the imagination, is addictive. Client relationships here are long term – one is almost tempted to say 'permanent'.

As well as strong links with ad agencies, Imagination has also had solid fastenings with engineers and architects. Buro Happold has put the stern disciplines of structural engineering at the service of Imagination's imagination, making flights of fancy into credible realities. While many art school graduates could think up this or that fantastic scheme, Imagination had the contacts to deliver. At the same time, Imagination's reputation has been enhanced by close association with distinguished architects. The influential, prophetic and exciting group of AA architects styling themselves Archigram expired in 1975, but not before it had provided stimulus to, and defined the aspirations of, an entire generation of architects who would later

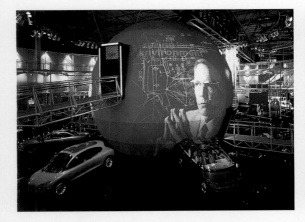

Far left, Ford's stand at the 1992 Birmingham Motor Show. The sides of the 10 m (30 ft) sphere were used as a projection surface. Left, the levitating dome used at the BT event Top Telco. Facing page, from left, projections for *The Music of Andrew Lloyd Webber* at Expo '92 in Seville; the Bone Walk bridge in 'Dinosaurs', a permanent exhibition at London's Natural History Museum; the logo of Millennium Central projected into the atrium of Imagination's Store Street offices.

be described as High-Tech. In 1989, Ron Herron, an Archigram founder, folded his practice into Imagination. The significance of this was twofold: first, it gave Imagination a new credibility among a community of architects who perhaps thought the smoke-and-mirrors stuff was a mite too insubstantial and a lot too flash. Second, it gave Imagination the best possible advertisement for itself: a landmark building in London's Store Street which Herron designed. He turned a huge redbrick Edwardian school into a genuinely imaginative conceit. No other design company anywhere has anything even half as impressive: a PVC-coated canvas roof six storeys up created a dramatic, light-soaked atrium. Herron said 'There are buildings worth saving, but we usually seem to be saving them for negative reasons – because we think the replacements would be worse – rather than for their own merits'. Vertiginous steel walkways connected the separate blocks of the old school. Bricks were painted white, *Ficus benjamina* was planted. It was a brilliantly confident exercise which immediately raised the level of Imagination's game yet again. Store Street oozes credibility and authority in a way few rivals can imitate, but then Imagination has very few rivals.

It's a curious truth that the exhibition, that most simple, but also most effective, of communications devices acquired new force and relevance in the 90s. The more wired we get, the more valuable it is to bring people together in a designed environment where data, information, knowledge, persuasion, entertainment and opinion can be modulated by architectural space, theatrical gestures and creative lighting. The fact is, a conventional fly-tower counterweight system, 256-point typesetting, titanic photography, neat copywriting and beautiful, rare objects can still do many things a PowerPoint cannot. This was recognized not only by Ford and BT, as British Telecom became, but by a slew of private and public bodies who have benefited from Imagination's exceptional expertise and can-do competence. These included MCA Universal, Pearsons, The European Commission (for whom Imagination built a pavilion at the Seville Expo of '92), Cadbury Schweppes, Disney, the Natural History Museum, Andrew Lloyd Webber and Time Warner.

When John Major's government created a National Lottery and a Millennium Commission as morale-boosting remedies for national recession, Imagination was a leading candidate to design and even operate a national celebration of the year 2000. For Withers the opportunity to 'do' the Millennium was the most complete expression of what Imagination stood for and would, besides, also be the most complete advertisement imaginable. The entire staff, about half a million pounds and a persuasive personal belief system were put into a pitch that impressed and astonished everyone who saw it.

It was not merely a flip chart and spiral-bound document presentation, but a brilliant *coup de théâtre*. Withers spoke for twenty minutes without notes or hesitation. Drawing on all that transmogrificational expertise acquired in pitches, shows and expos for hard-nosed multinationals, taking windows out of Versailles and making Castle Ashby melt into air, for instance, Withers astonished his audience. Imagination took over an entire room and in it created an exquisite, bespoke environment. It was blue and metal with sharp, modern furniture. Video screens flickered knowingly: a movie, somewhat sentimental, was made showing a prototype Billy Elliott boy child visiting the HQ of Millennium Central (in fact Imagination's Store Street offices). The point, Withers insisted, was not to imitate the Great Exhibition of 1851, but to make an analogy of it.

What Imagination proposed was a 'living and evolving millennium destination'. The creative idea was entirely the opposite of a didactic, authored, centralized exhibition in a single location. Instead, the proposal was that during 1996, 'Millennium Spheres' should be set up to travel around the country, both to stimulate and to gather local activity. At the end of this itinerary, they would arrive at the exhibition site – 'Millennium Central' – where they would be attached to an ambitious structure of ten separate pavilions. It was fundamental to the Imagination concept that this destination should be … Birmngham.

Not only was this idea conceptually daring – indeed, properly *imaginative* – but it had the additional advantages of giving adequate time to develop generous levels of corporate sponsorship, while being genuinely national and with the potential for wholly eclectic content. From its experience of trade shows and expos, Imagination was able to write a budget that was within the range of possibilities offered by the Millennium Commission grant. Millennium Central, as envisaged by Imagination, was not to happen, though. The reason? Even after Withers had been persuaded to move his scheme to Greenwich, delays in appointing a credible operator made Imagination's original creative

proposals undeliverable, and the company decided to step back from the project.

Instead, the later 90s brought a new and consistent stream of commercial exhibition business, including two zones in the Dome, 'Talk' for BT and 'Journey' for Ford, both commissioned and controlled by the two sponsors. With its flurry of privatizations turning into a torrent of Initial Public Offerings, the booming Telecoms Media Technology sector has created a worldwide demand for roadshows as perhaps the most effective communications tool in investor relations. It's a beguiling truism of the contemporary world that when Terra Networks, Swisscom or Deutsche Telekom need to communicate with their investors, they resort not to 512-gigabyte chips, DVD or broadband, but to the simple drama of theatre. Imagination has built the environments where the largest ever IPOs have been staged.

It is a truth often thought, but never very well expressed, that the nature of advertising is changing. The fragmentation of the once monolithic media into text messaging, digital-terrestrial, satellite, Internet, freesheet, direct mail, MP3 and brand experience makes national campaigns for all but commodity products look increasingly wasteful. Why, when only, say, 0.05 per cent of the entire population even has the potential or desire to buy a Porsche, advertise in a national medium claiming access to 20 per cent of the population? More accurate solutions are required.

At the same time, the actual structure of advertising agencies is being modified. Once the creative teams of advertiser and copywriter held a sort of queasy primacy. It is not that the creative content of advertising is declining, but that clients are tending to put less emphasis on end product, more on planning and definition. What agencies call 'planning', or what the rest of the world calls research, is at least as creative a part of the world of paid-for communications as writing a snappy copyline or art-directing a shoot. Moreover, conventional advertising is only one of many solutions available to the client, who is now susceptible to many different approaches. Advertising is no longer just an interpretation of an established idea, but is ever more concerned with thinking about what a product should mean. Imagination – which can do you a roadshow, make you a film, script an ad, shoot it, design you a building or publish a book – is perfectly poised to consolidate a very fluid business. It is in the middle of what you might call an entrepreneurial riot.

The potential for exhibitions and events is huge. What in future will be known as 'The Tate Modern Effect' is the governing principle here. The more wired we get, the faster we move, the more we interact with electrons, the greater and more ravenous becomes the public's appetite for being in touch with beautiful and interesting objects and ideas placed in a creatively designed environment. Ford's last motor show stand was not simply a display of shiny cars, but an event which blurred the distinctions between sales patter and philosophy, between commerce and culture. We live in a world, as Felipe Fernandez-Arnesto says 'of expanding information, while wisdom, learning and scholarship stagnate or contract'. The cleverest companies realize that and will probably employ Imagination at some time in the future.

The possibilities for Imagination are enormous. So far as I can tell, no-one working there acknowledges any limits to future developments or how the business might grow. Imagination keeps on re-inventing itself and building on the re-invention. But it's prudent to write a word of caution: the jungle of brands and corporations where Imagination is a big stalking beast is under attack from some very articulate and persuasive voices. You don't have to be a flat-earther or tree-hugger to see the sense in, say, the argument of Naomi Klein, the *Toronto Star* journalist, who in her book, *No Logo,* says that the multinationals are brand bullies who have militarized the opposition. Or Malcolm Gladwell, whose *Tipping Point* argues that consumer behaviour is irrational and, therefore, that commercial communications are arbitrary and unscientific. Well, maybe. But the one way to prove that you have imagination is to keep on changing it. A definition of intelligence and, perhaps, of creativity is that it is 'behaviour which is adaptively variable'. If the consumers' interest in brands dwindles and is replaced by an enthusiasm for more austere intellectual values, then Imagination with its vast portfolio of diversified talent can adapt and vary. You just have to do the unexpected. It has been reported that Andy Grove of Intel, the least compromised of Silicon Valley businesses, sacks himself everyday so that he can arrive the following morning and say to himself 'Gee! I'm new to this job! Let's remove all the old assumptions about how to run this business and start again'.

Imagination is a little like that. Because we have done things that way in the past is a very good reason for doing them differently in future. Gary Withers may have started breeding angel fish and packaging

weddings, but now his firm is designing shops for Space NK and lighting the Lloyd's Building, presenting the 'Dinosaurs' exhibition in London and creating television programming for corporate clients. In 2000 it opened its first permanent brand facility, the Guinness Storehouse in Dublin, which with its combination of retail and leisure spaces, public exhibitions and business facilities, bricks and mortar and smoke and mirrors, might be seen as the coming together of all that Imagination has learned from its work in exhibitions and events over the years. The analytical will see a certain pattern there, but Withers has insisted that there was no Grand Plan. Just energy, commitment, a taste for the theatrical and an inclination to think big. As Pascal knew, the very last thing you should do is decide what comes first. With no plan and no inhibiting Big Idea, Imagination has shown how far you can go by being daring. Imagination is huge and will get bigger. Why Imagination has succeeded when its contemporaries have grown exhausted or parodic is hard to say except in the words of the writer Christopher Morley, as they appeared in Rosser Reeves' classic *Reality in Advertising* (1961): 'If you go directly to the heart of a mystery, it ceases to be a mystery and becomes only a question of drainage'.

Drainage may be the answer. It is often said that the mark of a successful event is one where the necessity of car parking and the desirability of lavatories have not been over-looked. Imagination has the practical sense to know about parking and plumbing, but it has other things as well, notably a sense of theatre, a complete refusal to compromise and an inclination towards the unexpected. It is not just a matter of thinking the unthinkable, it's one of building it as well. Ultimately, if you can imagine it, you can do it. And they do.

Facing page, left to right, Journey, sponsored by Ford; Talk, sponsored by BT; stage set for a Deutsche Telekom investor relations roadshow. Left, interior and exterior views of the Guinness Storehouse.

Inform

Designing to inform is not about being didactic;
it's about making spaces in which people can make
up their own minds.

Journey, London, 1999

Architecture and exhibition design for a walk-through visitor attraction at the Millennium Dome, depicting the past, present and future of transportation.

Journey was one of the fourteen themed pavilions in the Millennium Dome, devoted to travel and transportation in all its forms. In December 1998, Imagination was commissioned by the zone's sponsor, Ford Motor Company Limited, to design, construct and curate the exhibition, as well as the building in which it was housed. Ford's brief to Imagination echoed the aims expressed by the New Millennium Experience Company (NMEC), the Dome's operator: the zones should reflect our past as well as the present, and should show how we as individuals can make a difference in the future. Imagination proposed that Journey should not just focus on different modes of transportation but consider the reasons why we travel. By increasing visitors' awareness of the importance of travel in our lives, the zone could show that the future was not predetermined, but would be decided by the choices that millions of individuals make every day. While the zone had to inform, however, it also had to avoid the ever-present danger of appearing didactic; success depended on providing visitors with enough information to make up their own minds. Furthermore, the information had to be presented in a way that was entertaining – the contents, like the building itself, would compete with thirteen other zones for attention and visitors. As a national exhibition, the Dome had to appeal to as broad a cross-section of the population as possible. The NMEC identified three types of potential visitor to each of the zones – graded 'paddlers', 'swimmers' or 'divers', based on the strength of their interest in the subject – and Imagination endeavoured to tailor the content of the zone so that it was both informative and entertaining at any of those three levels of immersion.

The architecture of the zone was complicated by the 2,200 sq m (23,670 sq ft) 'footprint' allotted to it: the site was divided into three discrete parcels of land, separated by ground level walkways and emergency vehicle access routes. The zone sat between the Dome's internal ring road, at ground level, and the raised promenade level circling the central arena. Regulations forbade the construction of exhibition floors above the promenade level, and consequently, much of the zone's content was housed in a mezzanine level built under the overhang created by the raised walkway. Due to the curvature of the ring road, visitors could not get a complete view of the zone's 80 m (260 ft) length, so an icon tower, known as the Control Tower, was added to the plan. As well as identifying the zone from a distance, the tower allowed vertical circulation through the exhibition and served as a point of orientation for visitors within it. The footprint and consequent shape of the building dictated that visitors would have to pass over three storeys and through the three buildings, via bridges and the mezzanine floor, to get from one end of the exhibition to the other. Combined with the need to throughput up to 3,000 visitors an hour, this suggested a linear narrative structure for the exhibition. Consequently, the visitor passed chronologically through the past, present and future of travel. Throughout the zone, a rich, multi-layered presentation allowed information to be either cursorily scanned or examined in depth. The use of mixed media enhanced intellectual and sensory stimulation: film and multimedia were combined with graphic displays and photography to augment the presentation of static and interactive exhibits, while careful control of sound, lighting and temperature levels helped to create a fully immersive experience.

Facing page, above, computer renderings of the structure. Below, the fins of the zone.

12

ive Jump Float S
Wander Rush Da
Sprint Glide Ska
ide Sail Row Rac
ly Cycle Meander

Flat out

Journey *Ford*

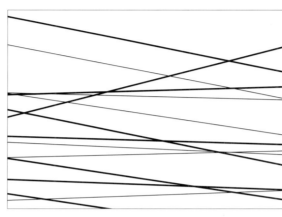

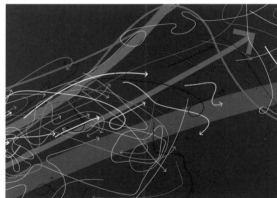

Top, examples of the zone's graphic language, applied to display panels and website. Above, explorations of a graphic language based on the physical structure of the zone and representations of movement.

Architecture
The zone was over-arched by thrusting aluminium-clad fins, themselves reminiscent of a moment of motion, frozen in time. The fins were impressive in scale – up to 60 m (197 ft) long, extending to a height of 26 m (85 ft) above ground and with a surface area of 2,000 sq m (21,520 sq ft) – but in order that they should not appear ephemeral, a solid visual anchor was needed. This was to be the angular box that is the heart of the zone.

Graphic language
The graphic language developed for the zone was informed in a large part by Imagination's research into representations of motion, from the random trajectories of colliding particles to the blur through a train window and the churning wakes of ships. The colour palette began with Ford's blues and greys, to which were added the vivid accent colours of red and yellow. The typeface used throughout the zone and its sundry communications was Univers, chosen both for its qualities as a clear, legible typeface and its track record in airport, railway and road signage.

Left, computer renderings of the zone.
Facing page, digital wire frame drawing showing the internal structure of the fins.

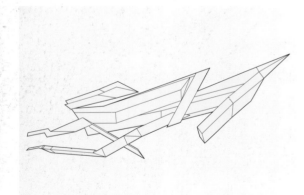

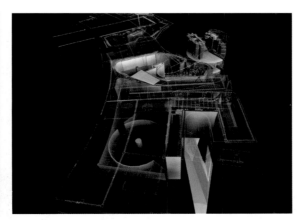

14

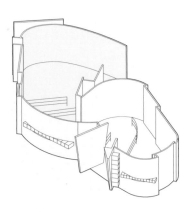

Film

Visitors entering the zone were met by a series of screens on which a film was playing. Titled *eMotions*, the film explored the reasons why, rather than how, we travel. The film presented a series of surprising images – a Buddhist monk against the high-tech backdrop of Stansted Airport, a priest peering from the back of a yellow cab at the mean streets of New York, a jogger with a prosthetic limb – simultaneously demonstrating the variety and universality of the travelling experience.

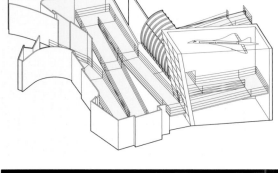

Ramps

The visitors' 'journey about journeys' began on a series of switchback ramps leading up to the mezzanine level. On the walls and suspended in the air overhead was a multi-layered presentation of statements, facts, quotes, artifacts and models which told the story of our travelling development from the Stone Age onwards. Twists and turns in the ramp were inevitable, given the restrictions of the space. Taking account of this, the design of the exhibition on the ramp was intended to make the journey feel like a constantly evolving series of revelations. Punctuation points such as a large-scale model of Concorde and a working steam engine piston section, both with 'sound tracks',

were designed to keep attention levels high and offer glimpses of what lay ahead. As the visitors moved 'through time' they arrived at the congestion of the present day, symbolized by the 'Chaos Corridor', an enclosed ramp whose glass sides encased strobing neon tubes, while overhead a series of monitors played a mixture of static interference and footage of congestion and transport chaos. Disoriented, visitors stepped into a large, circular environment, painted white and with a blue light wash. 'Decompression' marked the end of the exhibition's consideration of the past and present of travel, and the beginning of its discussion of possible futures.

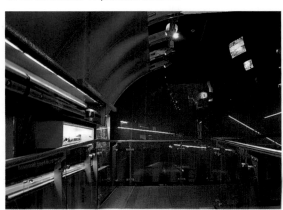

Top, diagram of the film screening room and stills from *eMotions*. Above and facing page, the ramps ascending to the mezzanine level. Left, the Chaos Corridor.

Above, the Chaos Corridor in which monitors showed films of transport chaos cut with static interference. Facing page, Decompression, the transitional point between the exhibition's consideration of the past and its exploration of the future.

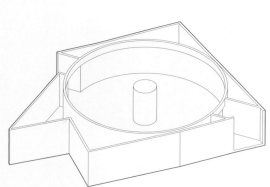

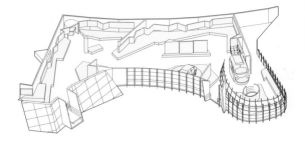

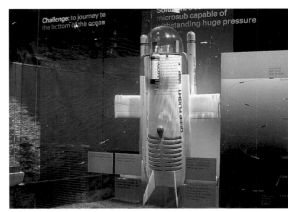

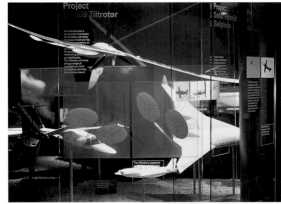

Above, future technologies exhibits in 'Journeys of Innovation'. Left and facing page, exhibits included the latest man-powered 'vehicles', from in-line skates to running shoes. Below, the multimedia interactive 'Four Futures' presented four possible scenarios for our transportation future, based on the testimony of 'expert witnesses', and asked visitors to register their own views. Overleaf, Journey viewed from the central arena of the Millennium Dome.

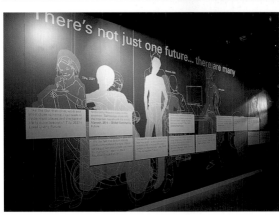

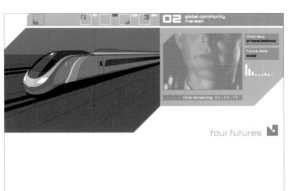

Journeys of Innovation

In 'Journeys of Innovation', exhibits and commentary examined some of the ways in which designers, governments and scientists might shape future journeys on land, sea and air. In addition to static and interactive exhibits, the exhibit on used a variety of media including graphics, film, multimedia and holography to describe prototype vehicles and transportation technologies. Based on this information, visitors were asked to register their views on how we might better manage our travel requirements in the future.

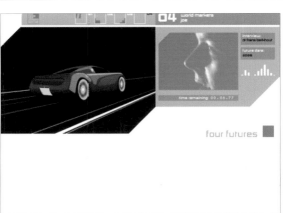

Dinosaurs, London, 1992

A permanent exhibition at the Natural History Museum, exploring the latest scientific discoveries on the lives and behaviour of dinosaurs.

The commission to build 'Dinosaurs', a permanent exhibition in the Natural History Museum, came at a significant time in the development of exhibition design, and played a role in proving that the mixed-media, 'interpretive' approach to museum curation could be done successfully. The museum had generated some controversy over earlier efforts to modernize its approach to the display and explanation of scientific material, but was firm in its conviction that the role of the modern museum was to make the subject matter accessible and entertaining as well as accurate and true. Its brief to Imagination stated: 'this is to be an exhibition that visitors can use to inform themselves about dinosaur natural history, and not merely a display of impressive specimens.' Although the exhibition was targeted at people of all ages, with every level of understanding, it was pitched specifically at adults over the age of fifteen, with a minimal knowledge of the subject. Educational and psychological evidence suggests that the best way to communicate information to this target audience is through a process of 'active discovery' – allowing visitors to make connections for themselves. The museum's brief stipulated that the gallery should blend information with experience and entertainment, with the exhibits arranged in such a way that 'visitors, while not feeling forced into compliance, can easily see the intended order of viewing and follow it automatically. The nature of the science to be included is such that it does not form a cumulative argument, but the developers should imagine the content as a simple story line where the topics flow naturally from one to the next.' Imagination responded to the brief by outlining its own aims: to make the exhibition entertaining without undermining the credibility of the museum as a scientific institution; to display the collection of dinosaurs in a dramatic yet understandable way; and ultimately to counter visitor perceptions of dinosaurs as a slow, stupid, 'failed' species by drawing on latest discoveries and thinking about their lives.

The Natural History Museum, designed by Sir Alfred Waterhouse, is a Grade-1 listed building, a classic example of high Victorian architecture. Its director had been threatened with jail by English Heritage over alleged amendments to the building during the construction of the Ecology Gallery a year earlier, and any interference with the fabric of what had been, since 1885, the Bird Gallery, was strictly forbidden. In the event, and having decided that a self-contained 'black box' exhibition would be undesirable and inappropriate, Imagination took the opposite route, advising the museum that the existing architecture would make the perfect backdrop to an exhibition on dinosaurs, and thus, as much as possible should be made of it. On an early site visit, the designers had discovered Waterhouse's original columns, complete with terracotta animal mouldings, hidden behind some unsightly panelling. Imagination stripped the cladding from the columns and reinstated Waterhouse's original oak floor, restoring the original axial views through the 80 by 15 m (262 by 49 ft) gallery. Into this space was introduced a dramatic contrast in the form of the Ron Herron-designed Bone Walk, a 70 m (230 ft) high-tech bridge built of gunmetal and perforated steel. Although the 'spinal' bridge visually echoed the dinosaur skeletons suspended from it, its principal purpose was practical rather than aesthetic: it was a means of carrying people from the entrance of the gallery to the far end without taking up too much floor space, allowing visitors an overview of the exhibits before making their way back through the room. In the first year of opening, 1.5 million visitors made their way along the bridge, past the suspended skeletons of dinosaurs into an animatronic recreation of a scene from 100 million years ago; here three Deinonychus were feasting on the remains of a dead Tenontosaurus. The animated tableau followed a 'script' of sound and movement based on behaviours of contemporary pack-hunting animals. The comparison with extant species formed the basis of the exhibition. Visitors coming in were asked the question 'Were dinosaurs like animals living today?' In a seamless display of text, still and moving pictures, aspects of dinosaurs' lives were compared to those of modern animals under titles such as 'the world around them', 'attack and defence', 'families, groups and loners'.

As the gallery is in a Grade-1 listed building, even light fittings could not be attached directly to the walls. Working around the restrictions, Imagination's lighting designers created a scheme that mixed architectural with theatrical lighting, and large-scale effects with intricate detailing. The stripped-back pillars are up-lit by floor-recessed uplighters which bring the terracotta animals crawling over them into relief, as well as bouncing ambient light off the ceiling. Information panels are lit by low-voltage spotlights cantilevered from the panel supports, with the angles carefully calculated to avoid glare. The suspended dinosaur skeletons are picked out by heavily baffled 300 watt spotlights hung from the bridge, while other floor level uplighters add texture and shadow to the bones. Each specimen is identified by an electro-luminescent panel with glowing lettering, designed and built by Imagination's research and development department. The more delicate exhibits, housed in glass cases, are cross-lit by small fibre-optic spots, thereby avoiding the need to open the case and expose the exhibits every time a bulb fails. Suspended above the animatronic dinosaurs, a theatrical lighting rig creates a moody effect, while a pre-programmed dimming system shifts the emphasis between the animals in time with their movements.

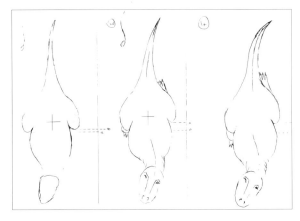
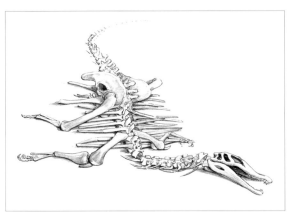

Above, sketches made in the course of research.
Below, clockwise from left, the exhibition under
construction; lighting brings carvings on the terracotta
columns into sharp relief; electro-luminescent display
panels; view from the bridge; dinosaur model;
model of hatching dinosaur eggs.

Below, sketch diagram for an animated sequence
depicting the feeding patterns of dinosaurs. Facing page,
view down the Bone Walk bridge.

Experience, worldwide, 1995

A visual anthology of contemporary art, design and architecture, published to illustrate the power of experiential communication.

Recognizing that the large-scale corporate exhibitions, conferences and events that had grown and sustained the company in the 1980s were not likely to remain a firm foundation for the business long into the 1990s, Imagination began to explore new opportunities. Brand-building was at the time starting to occupy a significant proportion of corporate consciousness, as The Brand was increasingly promoted by such leading business thinkers as Tom Peters as a company's most valuable asset. In 1993, Imagination set up a new department, the Brand Development Group, to consider how the company's multi-disciplinary creative resource might be used for the strategic building of brands. While the group developed new communications concepts for sale to new or existing clients, it habitually collected photographs of contemporary art and design work from around the world. In this collection, the designers believed they could see an increasing tendency emerging on the part of artists and designers to seek to communicate through sensory experience. Brands, they believed, could communicate in the same way. By the time the group was dissolved in 1995, 'Brand Experience' had become Imagination's main offer. The company had also made a conscious decision: that it would not attempt to make brand experience its own novelty sales pitch but instead would encourage its development as a major market, comparable to

the advertising or corporate identity industries. As part of this process, the company decided to publish a book featuring the work and concepts that had inspired the Brand Development Group over the years. The book, they hoped, would be neither a visually-led marketing manual nor a business-orientated design anthology but an indeterminate hybrid, which would inspire other designers, their clients and consumers with enthusiasm for experiential communication.

Edited by three members of the Brand Development Group, Sean Perkins, Adrian Caddy and Ralph Ardill, the book was published commercially by Booth-Clibborn Editions as *Experience: Challenging Visual Indifference Through New Sensory Experience*. It did not recognize conventional boundaries between creative disciplines, or between high and low culture. Work featured ranged from a fog forest park in Japan to monumental installations by the artists Christo and Jeanne-Claude, a Chiat-Day advertising campaign for Cable & Wireless, the architecture of Tadao Ando and Santiago Calatrava, the Rosemary Butcher dance company, U2's Zoo TV tour, the Pet Shop Boys' CD packaging by Mark Farrow, a new corporate identity for the Dutch police force by Studio Dumbar, artist Rachel Whiteread's *House* and the Vitra complex in Germany. The form of the book did not lend any sense of hierarchy or classification to these diverse projects.

The introduction carried a quotation stating that 'ideally a book would have no order to it and the reader would have to discover their own.' In planning *Experience*, the editors avoided predetermining its structure, and it was not until all of the spreads had been designed that the pagination of the book was decided, based on visual, textual, disciplinary, or conceptual links between projects or spreads that occurred to the designers and editors.

ARTIFICIAL NATURE

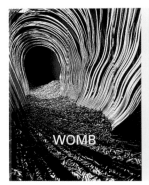

WOMB

LASER FOREST

JUST DO IT

EVERYBODY EXPERIENCES FAR MORE THAN HE UNDERSTANDS. YET IT IS EXPERIENCE, RATHER THAN UNDERSTANDING, THAT INFLUENCES BEHAVIOUR.'
MARSHALL MCLUHAN

Top, spread showing Seagaia, a leisure resort in Japan. Middle, left to right, spreads showing a 1992 Ford motor show stand, designed by Imagination, T-zone, an exhibition designed by Hiromi Fujii, Kei'chi Irie, Toyo Ito, Yutaka Saito and Shin Takamatsu, and NikeTown, designed by Nike Design. Bottom, the cover of *Experience*.

29

Something New, London, 1991

A dramatic temporary construction designed to house
BT's corporate identity launch.

Wolff Olins' redesign of British Telecom's corporate identity, in which the newly privatized firm gained a new 'piper' logo and was renamed BT, was intended to signify its repositioning as a global telecommunications leader, rather than a British utility company. Imagination was invited to pitch for the job of communicating the rationale behind the new identity to BT's senior managers, through an event, and to the rest of its staff through a cascade programme. BT had specified that the presentations to senior managers should be made by its Chairman, Sir Iain Vallance. Recognizing that the winning solution would most likely be the one that took Vallance away from his desk for the shortest possible period of time, Imagination decided that the event must take place within BT's corporate headquarters in Newgate Street, London. An inspection of the venue showed that there was no single room big enough to host the event. Attention settled on the atrium running up through the core of the building, but there was not enough flat floor space to seat 450 people.

The solution, however, was overhead; Imagination's proposal was to construct a 450-seat theatre suspended eight storeys up in the airy void of the atrium. Imagination worked with structural engineering consultants Buro Happold to overcome the challenges presented by building an auditorium in the air. The severe point loads coming down the eight storeys onto the ground floor, which itself was above five basement levels, were picked up through each of the basement floors with huge props. Above ground level, the designers were unable to fix anything to the marble walls of the atrium, and hence the entire nine-storey construction was in effect self-supporting, a platform on stilts, tensioned against various pieces of the building's structure, but not actually bolted anywhere. To provide adequate access, Imagination built a new entrance in the side of the building, which was later made permanent. Visitors arriving on the ground floor entered an exhibition on BT before proceeding to the auditorium via ramps, stairs and crawler lifts, all of which were specially installed. Construction and the installation of all supporting technology had to be done at night over a ten-day period to avoid disruption to the working building. Dismantling the structure took a mere four days. The auditorium itself was configured for presentation in-the-round. Suspended over the stage were rows of televisions, which along with projection screens lining the walls carried both still and moving images. Cameras relayed the action live from within the auditorium and, during question-and-answer sessions, in live feeds from other BT locations around the country. Live footage of the presentation was fed through an on-site studio, switching back out to the Telecom Tower and then beamed to BT locations around the world by satellite.

Above, the auditorium under construction, eight storeys up in the atrium of BT's Newgate Street premises.

Photography Bank, worldwide, 1998

Packaged in translucent plastic with a product description clearly printed on the front, the purpose of this photography resource, created by Imagination's in-house photography department, could not have been more apparent.

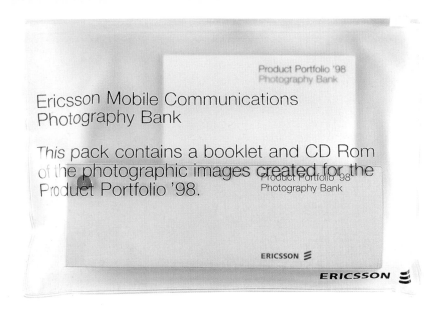

This is Your Brand, worldwide, 1997

Tasked with communicating the values of the Ericsson brand to its employees worldwide, Imagination designed a book which drew comparisons between products and situations familiar from everyday life with the language and tactics of brand management.

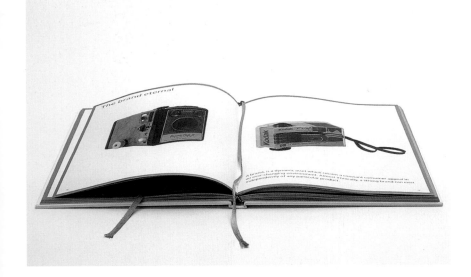

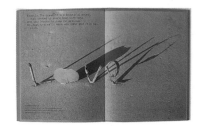

Earthquest, London, 1995
Concept for a Natural History Museum installation.
The process of travelling to the Earth Galleries via escalators
and the Museum's atrium would become a journey
through geological time, preparing the visitor for what
lay ahead.

Future Technologies Environment, Barcelona, 1997

Ford's exhibition stand at the Barcelona Motor Show featured a 15 m
(45 ft) frosted glass tunnel, onto which six interactive multimedia
animations showcasing Ford's concepts for automotive safety devices
of the future were back-projected.

Predators, London, 2001
The posters designed to support this Natural History Museum
exhibition on the behaviour of predatory animals make a
bold graphic feature of the animals' mechanisms for attack
and defence – teeth, horns and camouflage.

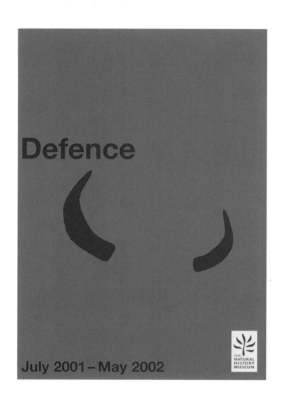

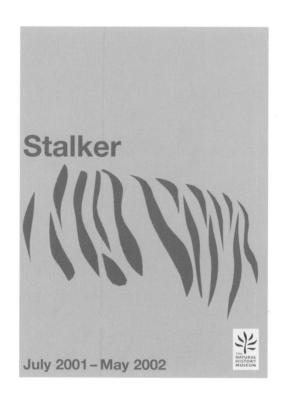

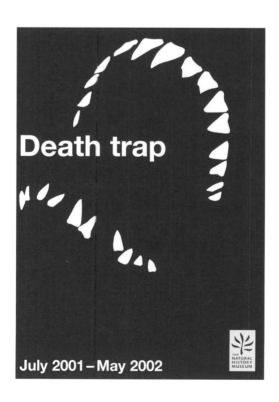

The Right People
Perspective: Sean Perkins

'Imagination is like a little Bauhaus; some people are doing great TV work, somebody else is creating a piece of multimedia, and somebody else is building a great piece of architecture. It just needed to be better about everything, and we had the opportunity with Brand Development to really push to get the best out of everybody.'

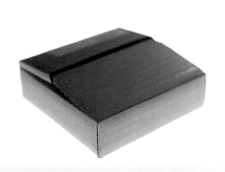
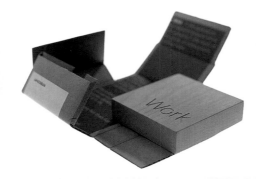

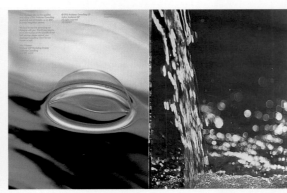
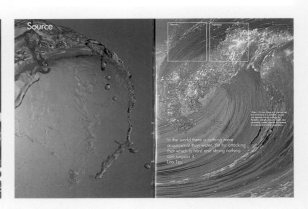

Above, top row, invitation to the launch of Work, a new range of Intercraft furniture. Above, bottom row, corporate brochure for Andersen Consulting.

Graphic designer Sean Perkins worked in corporate identity at Wolff Olins and Cartlidge Levene before arriving at Imagination in 1993. At the company he was a founder member of the Brand Development Group, charged with thinking about and reacting to the changing world of brand marketing. He left in 1995 to found his own design consultancy, North.

'Gary Withers claims that aggressively recruiting high-performance weirdos, whether or not there's a specific job opening, is essential,' wrote management guru Tom Peters in his book *Liberation Management*. 'Withers figures if the person is as interesting as he thinks, she or he will eventually find something clever to do that will vault the growing firm to the next plateau.' As Withers himself puts it, 'I've always looked for people who are interesting. I don't mind where anybody comes from, or what they do, or what they have been doing. If they fit, they fit.'

As the company evolves in response to new challenges and opportunities, the departments and facilities that are added are created around talented individuals with the capacity to catalyze growth and change. Withers cites as an example Andrew Bridge, 'an absolute inspiration', and later a double Tony Award-winner for his lighting of *Phantom of the Opera* and *Sunset Boulevard*, who was the nucleus of Imagination's lighting design department, growing it over twelve years to the point where it could tackle projects such as the lighting of the Lloyd's Building and the Hoover Building.

In 1993, Withers again recognized the need for a new department, this time one that would strategically address the changing communication needs of major corporations in the era of the brand, and at the same time tackle what he perceived to be a growing 'sameness' about Imagination's creative work. The solution was the Brand Development Group, into which Adrian Caddy, later Imagination's creative director, and Ralph Ardill, later marketing director, were transferred, and for which two outsiders, graphic designer Sean Perkins and magazine editor Stefano Hatfield, were recruited.

For Sean Perkins, the invitation to join the group was 'just the most fantastic job proposition ever. There was this opportunity to go in and talk to massive potential clients about what they should be doing, coming up with ideas for them before they even asked you – thinking for them proactively.' In the second part of the group's remit, too, he saw an exciting opportunity. 'In a romantic way,' he says, 'Imagination is like a little Bauhaus or Ulm School – there are so many disciplines and if you look around, some people are doing great TV work, and then somebody else is creating a piece of multimedia over there, and somebody else is building a great piece of architecture. It just needed to be better about everything – it needed to be the best at everything – and we had the opportunity with Brand Development to really push to get the best out of everybody.'

Perkins felt that Imagination's work at the time lacked some of the rigour and consistency of the corporate identity and information design worlds in which he had previously worked, and believed that his passion and experience could make a difference across the range of disciplines in which Imagination works. 'I feel that being a graphic designer is the best vocation,' he says. 'It's a privileged discipline because it means that you are an architect, you can be a fashion designer, you can be a TV director or a movie director, a photographer, illustrator, painter. And as a graphic designer I saw a way of injecting all of these other disciplines with a more European look and perspective on things.'

The group actively tried to win new business for Imagination through proactive approaches to potential clients with new communications concepts – game shows for Ford and branded clubs for Marlboro – and more conventionally through entering pitches for projects such as the environmental design for the Atlanta Olympics and the launch of the Sierra Nevada World Ski Championships. While it succeeded in winning some smaller projects, it found few takers for the grander, ground-breaking schemes that were creating so much excitement within the group and the wider company. Perkins ascribes this to the ideas being ahead of their time – a point of view corroborated by the company's later success in persuading clients to undertake similar communications programmes. In retrospect, he suggests, the projects effectively became test-runs in which the group honed its ideas on brand building, and established how Imagination's multi-disciplinary resources might be married with that strategic thinking to create a new approach to communication, which it christened Brand Experience: 'I think all of the things that we didn't win were part of a journey towards utilizing Imagination a lot better,' says Perkins. 'Focusing on problem-solving but delivering really excellent creative ideas, excellent results and a new standard of what the work should look like. Even though those particular projects didn't happen, in effect they happened eventually for other clients.'

At the time, however, Imagination recognized that it had to create an appetite for Brand Experience among marketeers if the ideas developed by the group were ever to be anything more than ideas. At Imagination, Perkins found himself in an unusual but essential role: 'My job was to inspire,' he explains, 'so I was bringing in books or photographs of things that I'd seen that I thought were really powerful, and it might have been something an artist had just done or it might have been a building in Tokyo.' That collection of material, in which the members of the group perceived an increasing tendency on the part of designers and artists to communicate through sensory experience, had informed much of its own thinking on Brand Experience. The obvious thing to do was to show it to the clients, which they did, in the book *Experience*. 'Most of what we do is education,' reasons Perkins. 'Presentations are all about getting clients to see things through your eyes. *Experience* was a tool we could use to say to clients or marketeers, "Look, all of these people can do it, you should be able to do it. Be brave, be bold." It was done to get people excited, to get them passionate.'

Looking back, Perkins recognizes that the group was always supposed to be about moving the frontiers of Imagination's business, and compares its activities to the research and development teams run by major corporations such as Nike,

Sony and AT&T. 'It was a big investment for Gary and I don't think we made enough money,' he remembers, 'but it was a bigger thing that we were doing and it took time; it wasn't going to happen overnight, and if we had won the first thing we pitched for, we would have failed, because we would have been so busy delivering it that we wouldn't have had the time to think about new ideas, new concepts, new directions.'

More than having the space to think without having to meet targets, or enjoying the facilities provided by Imagination, Perkins recognizes that it was the perfect mix of people that produced such far-reaching results in the small, short-lived group. 'Brand Development did become the whole company,' says Sean Perkins. 'The right people, in the right place, at the right time, helped to find a new direction for Imagination.'

Above, concept model of a proposal to the British Airports Authority (BAA) for a communications programme using lighting and projections on building site hoardings during the redevelopment of Heathrow Airport.

Entertain

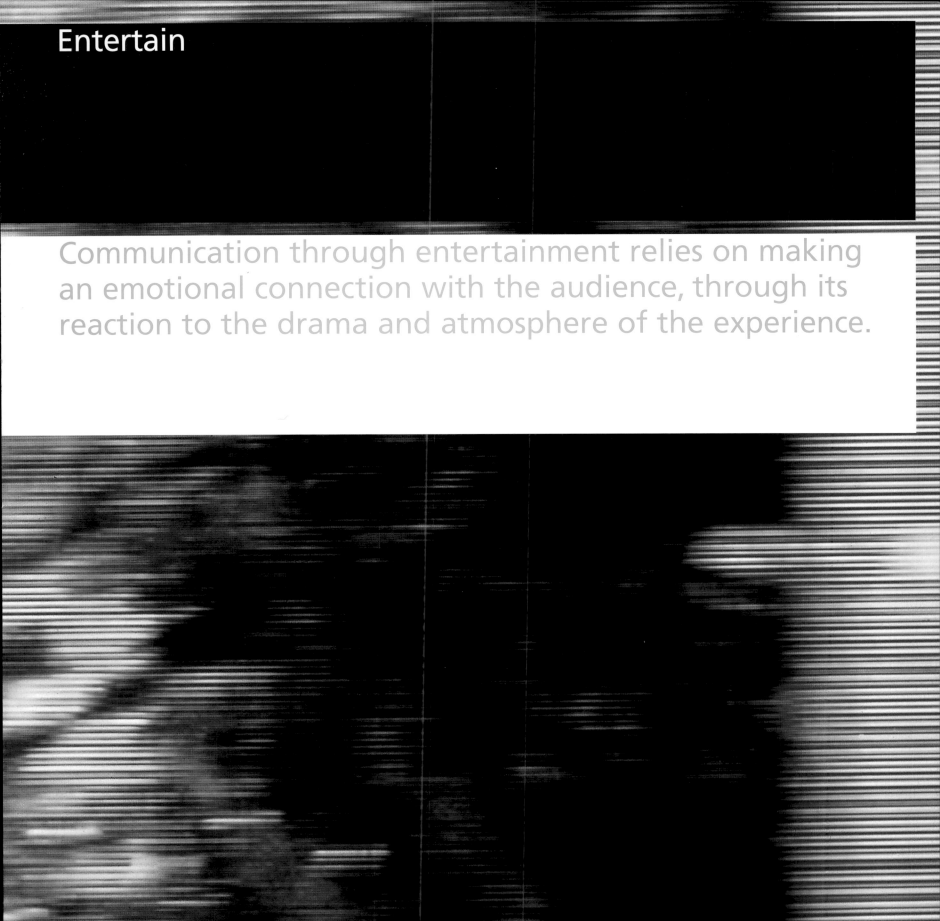

Communication through entertainment relies on making an emotional connection with the audience, through its reaction to the drama and atmosphere of the experience.

Schiphol Airport Interior, Amsterdam, 2000

A radical interior design scheme for the airport's Central Lounge extension, comprising retail and leisure elements.

Virgile & Stone's design for a new Central Lounge at Schiphol Airport represented a radical new departure in airport retailing. Schiphol is referred to by its owners as an 'AirportCity', providing 24-hour shopping and entertainment facilities as well as transport links, but the design solution created by Virgile & Stone, the interior design division of The Imagination Group, aimed to return some of the glamour and sophistication to airport travel by turning back the encroaching tide of commercialism which has made identikit shopping malls of many of the world's major airports. Instead, the new retail area has a department store style structure, in which the airport itself, rather than brand name retailers, is the apparent operator. The two-storey terminal extension, by architects Benthem Crouwel, provided 22,000 sq m (236,700 sq ft). Within this space, Virgile & Stone planned a shopping area of 3,700 sq m (39,810 sq ft) on level one and a food area of 2,200 sq m (23,670 sq ft) on level two. Within the Central Lounge, thirty individual retail outlets are operated by franchisees. As in a department store, the outlets dealing with each of the five key product groups – fashion, media, food, cosmetics and perfumes, liquor and tobacco – are clustered together, with three or four individual retailers working within each cluster. The designers opted to locate these retail 'pods' in the centre of the concourse on the ground floor, allowing a flow of passengers along broad paths past the shopping islands and providing unobscured views out onto the runway. On the upper level are a variety of bars and restaurants which overlook activity on the runways whilst maintaining a visual link with the retail area below.

Three vast organic structures, suspended in the air, dominate views through the space. These striking curved forms, between 30 and 40 m (100 and 130 ft) across, give the retail space a distinctive visual identity, but their presence was necessitated by more practical considerations: the decision to locate the retail pods in the centre of the space meant that some form of cover was required to house lighting and provide enclosure for security. Electronic gates, which close the three zones at night, form part of the roof structures by day. The canopies suspended above the pods draw inspiration from the language of aviation; their free-form geometry evokes the spirit of flight, whilst the aerodynamic forms are reminiscent of the contoured wings of the aeroplanes just metres away on the apron of the runway. Another parallel with flying machines is drawn through their internal structure: the skins and canopies utilize construction methods similar to early aircraft. Virgile & Stone worked with structural engineers Ove Arup to determine the matrix of the skeletal frames with curvatures in two planes. These frames are clad in plywood sprayed with a specially developed water-based metallic paint. The fibreglass cone which is at the heart of the retail area punctures the terminal roof and funnels light into the delicatessen below. Formed in one mould, the cone was constructed in an aircraft hangar on site and transported across the airfield at night.

Facing page, top, diagrams showing the aerodynamic forms suspended above the retail clusters. Bottom, the electronic gates provide security by night, but by day fold away as part of the roof structure, with incorporated lighting.

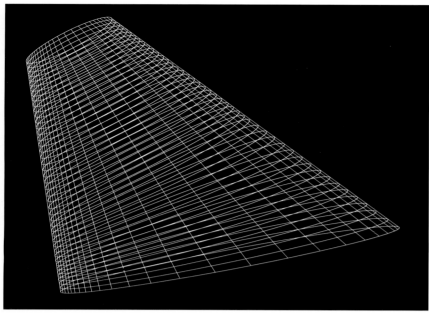

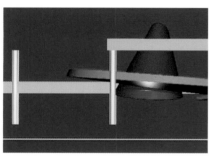

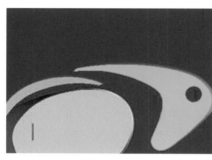

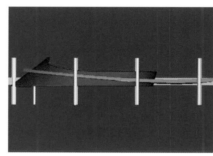

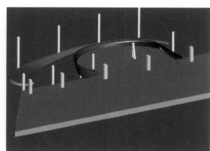

Above, Virgile & Stone worked with structural
engineers Ove Arup on the design of the suspended
canopies and the fibreglass cone. 3-D renderings of
the shapes were created from line drawings and
sketch models by Objectile, a digital architecture lab
specializing in non-standard design and manufacture.
Below, plans and models show the cone that pierces
the terminal roof, funnelling light into the delicatessen.
The fibreglass cone was craned in one piece into
the building.

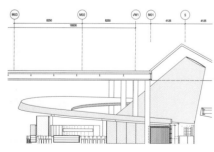

Above, clockwise from left, product display within the retail area; the Cone bar – the branding and graphics for the retail and food areas were also designed by Virgile & Stone; an aerodynamic form suspended within the space; the steel perimeter wall of a retail pod, with incorporated lighting. Overleaf, view through the Central Lounge.

Tate Modern Launch, London, 2000

A theatrical lighting and laser display designed to mark
the opening of the new art gallery.

Tate Modern stands on the River Thames in the heart of London, linked to St Paul's Cathedral by a new Millennium footbridge. Housing the Tate's collection of modern art, the new gallery was designed by the Swiss architects Herzog & de Meuron to occupy the former Bankside Power Station by Sir Giles Gilbert Scott. Imagination first became involved with Tate Modern early in its history, having proposed a series of illuminations to generate interest in the forthcoming attraction shortly after the new gallery was conceived in 1995. Five years later, when the time came to open the gallery, Tate Modern commissioned Imagination to design a light show that was 'simple and surprising', as opposed to crudely 'spectacular'. The show would be seen by 4,000 invited guests at the launch party, and would also be screened live by the BBC.

Imagination's solution was derived from the fabric of Tate Modern itself; throughout the evening, lasers picked out architectural details of the building, emphasizing the solidity and monolithic presence of the power station it once was and the new two-storey glass 'lightbeam' which runs the length of the 200 m (650 ft) roof. At the end of the party, and as the event 'went live' on television, the full sequence, involving lasers and coloured light washes, built up to the 'launch' of the building, signalled by the illumination of a lightbox at the apex of the chimney, designed by the architects with artist Michael Craig-Martin. The laser outlined first the chimney and then the two-storey glass lightbeam, forming a giant cross on the axes of the building, before a colour wave of light, from fifty arc wash luminaires, spread outwards across the glass lightbeam. A series of laser lines began to build up along the 99 m (325 ft) length of the chimney and a soft ripple effect, echoing the waters of the Thames below, started to play on the lightbeam. Meanwhile, dramatic colour changes were taking place, from deep green to deep blue, with reds and oranges as accent colours. Following the appearance of a laser line up the centre of the chimney, coloured blocks of laser light began to climb the chimney until, when they reached the top, the lightbox was illuminated for the first time. The sequence, which continued to play in a loop, lasted just four minutes, but the apparent simplicity of the display belied the complexity of the arrangements behind it: before any permissions were granted, Imagination had to produce a risk assessment document running to several hundred pages, guaranteeing, for example, that no works of art would be damaged by the lasers. The whole sequence was pre-programmed because of the second-by-second precision required, and lights, lasers and audio were managed by timecode, allowances having been made for sound delays across the large site. The scale of the area over which the display was being orchestrated also affected the nature of the display itself. The designers had to allow for two angles of view in their scheme: the TV cameras on the opposite bank of the river had a clearer view of the iconic forms identified by the laser, while the detailed colour textures created by the light washes were more visible to those at the foot of the building itself.

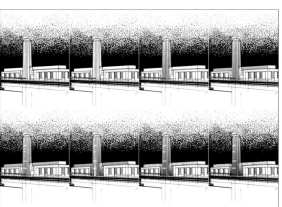
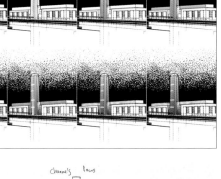

Concept sketches
Design concepts for the display began with the imposing form of the building itself, and playfully emphasized some of the iconic forms and finer details 'hidden' within the architecture. The impressionistic simplicity of the concept sketches contrasts with the technical precision required to mount such a show.

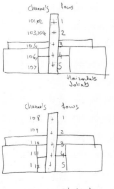

48

Above, elements of the four-minute lighting and laser sequence. Left, Imagination's interior lighting scheme for the right of the Tate Modern launch included the positioning of 1,000 wax candles in rows down the walls of the Gallery's Turbine Hall.

Above, the laser highlights the lines of the building
while colour washes fill the chimney and lightbeam.
Facing page, coloured blocks of light climb the chimney.

Guinness Storehouse, Dublin, 2000

A six-storey former brewing facility converted into a brand experience for Guinness, comprising an exhibition, public bars and staff training areas.

Since Imagination began to promote the concept of Brand Experience in the early 1990s, its thinking in this area has infused much of its core business in exhibitions, events and other forms of live communications. Its first opportunity to create a permanent brand experience, however, did not come until 1997, when the company was invited to pitch for the job of creating a new visitor attraction to replace the Guinness Hopstore, the brewer's popular tourist attraction in Dublin. Imagination was asked to consider two options in its proposal: the new attraction could either replace the Hopstore in its existing premises, or be located on the ground floor level of a nearby brewing facility that had lain empty for over a decade. Working in partnership with the Dublin-based architectural practice Robinson Keefe Devane, Imagination devised and presented a proposal to radically enlarge the scope of the project. The two firms suggested that the Guinness visitor experience should not only move to the disused fermentation plant, but should occupy all of its six floors, rather than just the ground level. The Guinness Storehouse, as it would be called, would include conference and training facilities as well as three public bars, a gallery and exhibition space in what Imagination described as a 'world first, world-class' brand centre, a physical space that would act as 'the ultimate expression of the character of Guinness'.

The Guinness Storehouse is designed to cater for up to a million visitors a year, divided into three key audiences. The largest audience by far is that of tourists, whose main interest is in the fixed experience – the exhibitions and bars. The Irish business community, including Guinness staff, uses the building's state-of-the-art conference and training facilities. The third audience, young Dubliners, come to the Guinness Storehouse for one-off events such as concerts, parties and exhibitions. In its proposal, Imagination stressed the importance of attracting local people as well as tourists. Imagination saw in the Guinness Storehouse an opportunity for Guinness not just to reconnect with its core market, but to give something back to the community with which its brand and history are inextricably linked. The company was convinced that the Guinness Storehouse should not just be a tourist attraction or a product showcase: 'Unlike most brand centres,' read its proposal, 'this is about cultural citizenship, not building corporate cathedrals.' The people of Dublin should be able to feel that they owned the home of Guinness in the same way that they feel ownership of the brand itself. Completed in 1904, the former fermentation plant in which the 'home, heart and soul of Guinness' would reside sits

in the heart of the sprawling St James' Gate brewery site, which itself dates back to 1759. Designed by AH Hignett of Guinness, with structural steelwork by Sir William Arrol, it was the first steel-framed building in Ireland. The architectural scheme developed by Imagination and Robinson Keefe Devane aimed to celebrate the history and unique qualities of the building. The steel frame that gives the building its historical significance was exposed and accentuated, while many of the pieces of industrial plant that had been left when the building ceased to function as a brewing facility were allowed to remain, either as characterful architectural details or as exhibits in their own right. The conversion was not just an exercise in conservation, however. Carved into the middle of the building, and running down through all six floors, Imagination created a glass atrium in the shape of a giant pint. Escalators running up through the atrium provide access to 15,790 sq m (170,000 sq ft) of floor space over the six levels, where the training and conference facilities sit side by side with a gallery, bars and the Guinness exhibition. The exhibition tells the story of Arthur Guinness, founder of the brewery, and enables visitors to discover what goes into making and distributing Guinness in a series of dramatic set pieces using three-dimensional exhibits, multimedia, film and large-scale graphics applied directly to the interior walls of the building. In addition to preserving original pieces of brewing equipment, the designers added features including an ingredients waterfall, which keeps 30 tonnes of water on the move, and a replica cooperage where visitors learn about the manufacture of casks: at one time, 250,000 barrels stood in the brewery's yard. Looking at the brand in a wider social context, the exhibition explores the nature of the relationship between Guinness and Ireland, and the way it has been transported around the world as the country's best known export. The visitor's experience at the Guinness Storehouse ends in Gravity, the bar on the roof – at the head of the giant pint. The circular bar is the highest point in the city of Dublin, and its glass walls allow 360-degree views across the brewery complex and beyond.

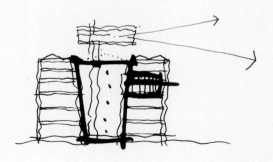

Above, early concept sketch showing the giant pint atrium. Facing page, the Ingredients waterfall.

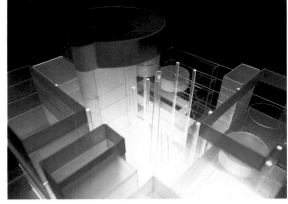

Above, concept model and drawing showing the giant pint atrium of the Guinness Storehouse. Left, aerial views of the Guinness Storehouse showing its location in the St James' Gate brewery complex in Dublin. Below, renderings of atrium and photograph showing the atrium under construction.

Above, left to right, rendering of Gravity, the rooftop bar; Gravity under construction; view of Gravity from beneath. Right, interior view of Gravity, which offers panoramic views of the city of Dublin. Far right, Gravity visible on the roof of the Guinness Storehouse.

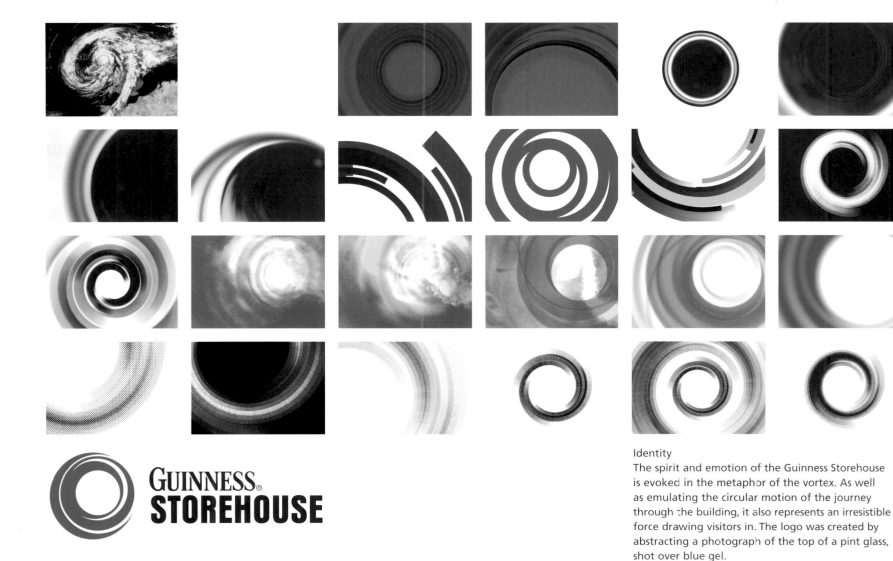

GUINNESS. STOREHOUSE

Identity
The spirit and emotion of the Guinness Storehouse is evoked in the metaphor of the vortex. As well as emulating the circular motion of the journey through the building, it also represents an irresistible force drawing visitors in. The logo was created by abstracting a photograph of the top of a pint glass, shot over blue gel.

WATER

THE WORD FERMENT COMES FROM THE LATIN 'FEVERE' MEANING TO SEETHE

SMELLS

BOILING AND HOPPING

250,000

01

POWER

ROAR OF ⇨ RAW

NOISE HEAT ⇨

MILLING – THE WHOLE PROCESS BEGINS BY COMBINING THE RIGHT PROPORTIONS OF MALT, FLAKED AND ROAST BARLEY.

⇦

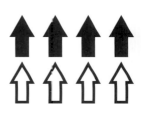

Top, sequence showing the development of the logo from the basic concept of a swirling vortex. Bottom, elements of the typographic language developed for the Guinness Storehouse.

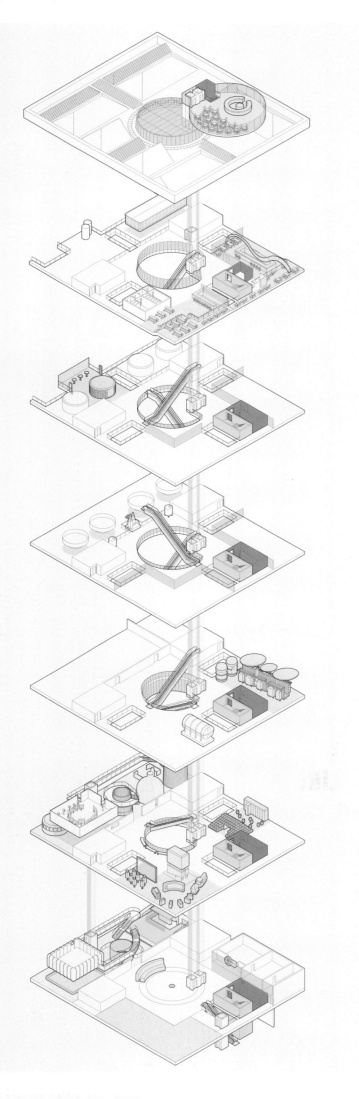

The visitor's journey

Although some areas of the Guinness Storehouse are reserved exclusively for staff training and general business use, the paying visitor's journey through the building takes them through all six floors, ending in Gravity, the rooftop bar, giving them a true sense of the scale of the attraction. Arriving at the ground floor, they enter a pre-show area in which a looped film sequence, screened in the round, frames questions that will be answered by the exhibits on the tour. The exhibition itself begins with Ingredients, which introduces the component parts of a pint of Guinness in a dramatic set-piece centred on a large-scale waterfall. The next exhibit, Arthur Guinness, tells the story of the brewery's foundation before the visitor moves to the first floor of the building through the giant pint atrium, progressing through exhibits on Brewing, Transport, the Cooperage, Life – which shows Guinness in a wider social context – and Abroad, documenting the brand's journey around the world. The second floor houses Advertising, the area of the exhibition in which Guinness' extensive advertising archive is displayed. The third floor is used for staff training but arriving on the fourth floor, the visitor enters Home, the area of the exhibition dealing with the relationship between Guinness and Ireland. The fifth floor houses two public bars, the Brewery bar and the Source bar while a third, Gravity, the rooftop bar, overlooks the glass-roofed giant pint and represents the end of the visitor's journey.

Left, exploded axonometric diagram showing the six storeys of the building. Above, the entry ticket to the Guinness Storehouse – a bubble of Guinness is encased in a clear plastic pebble. Below, the home page of the Guinness Storehouse website, Guinnessstorehouse.com. Facing page, interior view of the giant pint atrium.

Facing page, clockwise from top left, Transportation, which describes the means by which Guinness has travelled around the world; graphics in Transportation; the pre-show area at the start of the visitor's journey through the exhibition, in which a looped film of 'swirling and flaking' Guinness, overlaid with text questions, is shown in the round (270 degrees); detail of an exhibit in Brewing, the area of the exhibition illustrating the Guinness production processes.

This page, clockwise from top right, the Life area, which acts as a transition between the exhibition's consideration of Guinness as a drink and its exploration of the brand's relationship with the outside world; Arthur Guinness, a 360-degree projection environment supported by audio, props and theatrical lighting which tells seven stories about the brewery's founder and the history of Guinness; type applied directly to the building's interior walls; the Cooperage, in which visitors can learn about how casks are made; Brewing – many items of original brewing equipment were repurposed for this section of the exhibition.

Launch event

To launch the Guinness Storehouse, Imagination conceived 'Gravity', a show staged on three consecutive evenings within the building. The company collaborated with Jean-Pascal Lévy-Trumet, creative director of the opening ceremony of World Cup France '98, on the aerial and musical spectacular, performed before a total audience of 4,000 people over the three days. Set to a sound-track mixed by local DJs, the show featured a cast of twenty performers and utilized the entire building in an immersive display illustrating five themes: Attraction, Tension, Impact, Freedom and Equilibrium. Within the building's giant pint atrium, an aerial display featuring suspended performers flying through the space was set against a colourful backdrop of inflatables, lighting and projections.

Facing page and above, elements of 'Gravity', the show designed to launch the Guinness Storehouse. Overleaf, the Guinness Storehouse and Gravity, the rooftop bar, by night. The permanent architectural lighting scheme uses red light – inspired by the effect of shining light through a pint of Guinness – animated to suggest the distinctive appearance of a settling pint.

Sleeping Beauty Castle, Europe, 1992
A touring visitor attraction designed to generate publicity for the opening of the EuroDisney theme park.

The Sleeping Beauty Castle was a daunting and logistically complicated task, undertaken at very short notice and executed in a piece of industrial theatre which coupled panache with precision. The project had come out of the blue after Imagination was asked to cast an eye over a touring structure designed to generate 'front-page' news coverage across Europe for the opening of the new EuroDisney theme park, now Disneyland Paris. Having studied the plans, for an enormous pair of Mickey Mouse ears, housing a Disney experience, Imagination reported back to Disney that the scheme appeared unworkable, not least because the large ears would catch the wind like a sail, making the structure inherently unstable. Disney asked Imagination if it could come up with a workable alternative – in three days. Imagination proposed a half-scale model of the landmark Sleeping Beauty Castle at EuroDisney, which would contrast effectively with the surrounding architecture in the inner city locations it would visit. Around the arrival and construction of the castle at each location, Imagination foresaw three potential photo opportunities which would help to ensure the requisite front-page coverage: the assembly of the castle itself in front of a famous local landmark, a procession through the streets by Mickey Mouse and Minnie Mouse in an open-top car, and on the last night of its week-long residency, 'Fantasia in the Sky', a spectacular music, laser and firework show.

Having developed its plans over three days, Imagination had just fourteen weeks for the design, engineering and construction of the castle before it had to appear at Leipzig, the first location on its sixteen-city, thirty-week tour. Imagination worked with theatrical set-building specialist Kimpton Walker to design two demountable steel frames which would leap-frog each other across Europe so that the core structure could be erected before the cladding, equipment and cast arrived. The issue of windload, which had scuppered the earlier plan, was addressed by putting a water-filled raft in the castle's underfloor truss work. On top of the raft sat a pyramid-shaped steel frame, capped with a steel mast, onto which the cladding and turrets were bolted. The turrets, walls and roofs were constructed from a base structure of timber and plywood. The brickwork effect was created by applying various thicknesses of high-density foams and textures to the plywood and timber patterns; the appearance of stonework was achieved by applying plaster to the foam. Toilets, dressing rooms, and technical equipment for the sound, lighting and video were housed in four canvas-covered structures designed to look like medieval tents. The build

schedule began with a crew call at 6.00 am every Tuesday. By 8.30 am the pyramid trusses would be in position, and by 12.00 noon the support structure would be complete. The interior fit-up began at midnight and continued through the night. Work continued throughout the following day and night, until by 8.00 am on Thursday, the castle was ready for the first cast rehearsal. After the procession through the streets, the castle opened for business. Fifty people at a time entered for an audio-visual show lasting eight minutes, at the end of which Mickey Mouse appeared from a small housing in the middle of the interior structure, and led the audience outside to a meet-and-greet area while the next show was set up. Three days and over a hundred shows later, dismantling would start on Sunday afternoon, and by Monday night the crew had departed for the next venue. Due to the speed with which the project was initiated, only a few of the city-centre locations were booked at the start of the tour. Teams were sent ahead to reconnoitre suitable sites in the chosen cities, such as the Grand Place in Brussels, checking for level ground, the presence of a hard standing, photogenic landmarks, nearby hotels and restaurants for the crew, manhole covers for sewerage, and all the other things necessary to the smooth running of a touring show on a tight schedule. The last site negotiated was Expo '92 in Seville, Spain, where the castle remained until the end of the year, having generated millions of pounds worth of press coverage.

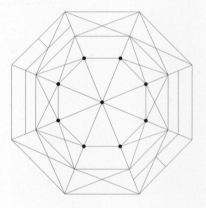

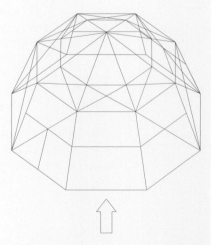

Above, diagram showing the steel frame onto which the decorative elements of the castle were bolted. Facing page, the castle under construction overnight in Hamburg.

Top, left, the audio-visual presentation inside the castle; middle and right, Mickey's appearance was the cue for 'Fantasia in the Sky' to begin. Below, the castle in Battersea Park, London (left) and Munich (right). Facing page, the castle at Expo '92 in Seville.

Lighting

A recurring lighting sequence brought the castle to life at night. Initially seen as if by moonlight, the castle was bathed in an eerie blue light, projected from lighting pods positioned around its base. Gobos produced a partially shielded light source, creating a dappled pattern on the main tower, which mysteriously started to move as the hourly appearance of Mickey drew near. Then, flickering lights, reminiscent of oil lights, came on before the illumination of impressive stained glass windows in the chapel at the rear of the castle. Detailed lighting was gradually added, emphasizing the three-dimensional form, depth and texture of the structure. Pale lavender floodlights cross-faded down to a wash of deep red light while star strobes positioned in nooks and crannies around the castle created the effect of many random flashes of white light. A series of 'pyro-flash' explosions was the cue for the clock to burst open, revealing Mickey against a background of fibre-optic stars, for the perfect photo-opportunity.

Skyscape, London, 2000
TV monitors encased in colourful pods were suspended within
a steel frame in the atrium of the Skyscape cinema at the Millennium
Dome. Designed to keep visitors entertained while waiting in line
for the next show, a specially produced film presented an amusing
take on the queuing experience while costumed performers
mingled with the crowd.

Adlab, UK, 1998

Advanced Design Laboratory – or Adlab – is a CD-ROM-based
multimedia experience designed to encourage more 13-year-olds
to study engineering-based courses at school. By enabling
them to design the car they could imagine driving in the
future, it introduces them to the kind of thinking practised
by designers and engineers.

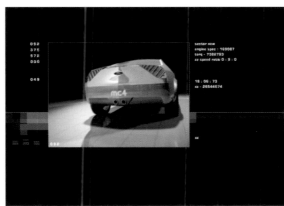

Puma Brand Film, Israel, 1997

Set to a specially composed soundtrack, 'Don't Deny Yourself', the
Puma brand film was intended to express the sense of liberation that
driving the car affords. A couple are seen driving away from a city,
its digitally rendered skyline visible in the background, and into the
wilderness. The location – Israel's Negev desert – provides a stunning
backdrop to the action while flamboyant characters, costumes
and props enhance the sense of celebration.

Live Entertainments, 1990–2000

In 1989, Imagination created a new subsidiary company, Imagination Entertainments, to harness the company's creative, production and technical resources to create live entertainments, both for conventional theatrical productions and for use in marketing communications initiatives created by the company.

Above, projections of core visual iconography from Andrew Lloyd Webber's shows created a dramatic backdrop for *The Music of Andrew Lloyd Webber* at Expo '92 in Seville. Left, the derelict Lyceum Theatre in London was restored for a New Year's Eve performance of a new pantomime, *Cinderella*, for an audience of Iveco Ford truck dealers (1990). Below, London's Alexandra Palace was the setting for Andersen Consulting's 1993 Partners' Conference. Taking 'Britain in the 60s' as its theme, the highlight of the evening was a performance by The Supremes against a synchronized backdrop of images from the period.

Above, a performance in the atrium of the Lloyd's Building depicted the history of the world's oldest insurance underwriting market in the year of its 300th anniversary in 1989. Right, performers from around the world participated in a celebration of Holiday Inn's 40th anniversary at the Royal Albert Hall.

Right, scenic design incorporating synchronized projections for the staging of *The Risen People* at the Gaiety Theatre, Dublin, by Playtime Productions and Hell's Kitchen, in 1994.

Left, a live Christmas broadcast from the Imagination Building by London Weekend Television featured highlights from a number of West End shows including *Copacabana*, a musical by Barry Manilow. For its West End and national tour, Imagination was commissioned by Apollo Leisure to develop a romantic scenic design evoking the spirit of the 1940s, as well as lighting, projection and sound design. Below, *The Music of Andrew Lloyd Webber* staged at St Paul's Cathedral in aid of the Lord Mayor's Appeal for St Paul's, 1994. Illuminations accentuated the architecture of the Cathedral, providing an imposing backdrop for the performance by a celebrity cast.

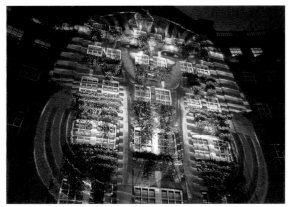

Above, BT's Livetalk '95 exhibition stand took its inspiration from a live TV entertainment format, using a diverse range of acts including music, comedy and dance to bring BT's core message to life. Left, the Imagination Building was transformed using lighting, projections, and several tons of sand to host a preview and media launch event for *Tutankhamun*, a new musical interpretation of the Tutankhamun story.

Once on This Island, London, 1994–5

London's Royalty Theatre was transformed into a Caribbean experience based on the musical *Once on This Island*, designed and produced by Imagination Entertainments, and sponsored by its client, Coca-Cola's Lilt brand. The performance was supported by bars and buffets offering West Indian food, a craft market and an after-show Cabaret Creole.

Cadbury Fantasy Factory, Bourneville, 1994

The Fantasy Factory is a visitor attraction for children, designed to bring to life all the fun of chocolate production. Theatrical techniques, interactive exhibits and animatronics combine to create the illusion of a fully functional factory, in which giant conveyor belts link the individual attractions while liquid chocolate bubbles and gurgles through pipes and vats.

BT Talktown, London, 1997

Outline proposals for the development of Talktown, a
unique environment fusing entertainment, education and
technology designed to communicate the BT brand.
The scheme also involved the creation of a circular elevator
that would carry visitors up the first half of the Telecom
Tower, providing panoramic views over London.

The Luxury of Time

Perspective: Lorenzo Apicella

'The need to resolve something before someone's going to make it tomorrow morning is actually very stimulating; you don't amble through it, you race through the project, and that energy can be very creative.'

Above, aspects of the Ford stand at the 1986 Birmingham Motor Show, with architecture by Lorenzo Apicella.

Architect Lorenzo Apicella spent two years in Houston, Texas, with Skidmore, Owings & Merrill, before joining Imagination in 1986 to lead major new architecture and design projects. He established his own practice, Apicella Associates, in 1988, whose work ranged from urban master-planning to the design of commercial buildings and interiors. In 1998 he joined the international multi-disciplinary design company Pentagram as a principal in the London office.

The Imagination offices are open and staffed around the clock, every day of the year. By day, the building is the hub of an extended network, co-ordinating activity around the world, alive with the comings and goings of staff, visitors, materials, equipment. By night, the apparent calm that descends belies the presence of a straggling few, buried in a basement editing suite, maintaining a lonely vigil in front of a screen or the cutting mat, scalpel in hand, one eye on the clock, mounting the presentation boards for tomorrow's meeting. The race against the deadline is as constant a factor at Imagination as in any newspaper office.

The reasons for the pace at which the company works are many: most obviously, Imagination actively positions itself as a company that can deliver at short notice, whatever the circumstances. Gary Withers defines the company's offer as 'the ability to come up with a creative solution that can be delivered quickly to the highest quality. That's where we've always scored on everybody else. We get there quicker.' The touring Sleeping Beauty Castle, designed, constructed and on the road in just fourteen weeks is a typical example of the type of challenge the company regularly invites. And the more Imagination delivers at short notice, the more its clients come to rely that it will. This pressure is compounded by the fact that there are no revised deadlines for the kind of work that makes up the bulk of Imagination's business; everything must go right on the day.

The unique demands of the kind of work in which Imagination specializes came as something as a surprise to architect Lorenzo Apicella, although the circumstances of his introduction to the company may have given him some inkling of what lay in store: 'My first contact with Gary was actually an interview at seven o'clock in the morning,' he remembers, 'because that was the only time he could make it.' Apicella, who had previously worked designing towers for Skidmore, Owings & Merrill in Texas, joined the company in 1986 to design two motor show exhibition stands, for Ford and Iveco. His brief was to push the boundaries of exhibition design. Offering a choice of routes through the space via a 50 m (165 ft) bridge, raised walkways, balconies and staircases, the Ford stand was essentially an architectural creation: 'My immediate thinking was that we were making buildings within buildings,' says Apicella. 'We were making "frames" that organized our environment to be as separate from the rest of the environment as possible, whilst relating to it in a strategic way. So I approached it in the same way that you might begin to make a building on a site in a city, looking at all of its primary, secondary and tertiary aspects – views to and from it and access to and from it and so on.'

One critical difference, however, was the length of time in which the two stands had to be designed and constructed. The urgency appealed to Apicella from the outset: 'It had to happen in a matter of months, so it was very exciting, compared to the pace one had been used to, where buildings take years to conceive of, define and then to actually construct.' The full implications of it did not dawn on him for a while, however: 'I remember working on these projects, and getting a call from Gary on a Sunday morning, saying "Look, I'm on site with the contractors, and they're saying that unless they get all of this information tomorrow, there's really going to be a problem about delivering these environments." I hadn't realized, because I wasn't used to that pace yet, that there was a need to do it *now*. I went into the studio, and twenty-four hours later I was still there. I'd been doing scale drawings all night. Gary came in the next morning at about six, checked what I was doing, got me some breakfast, and we met up with the production guys at about nine o'clock.'

But deadlines are not the only reason that Imagination stretches itself to the limits of its capabilities time and again. From its earliest days, the company's growth has been driven by accepting 'impossible' challenges. Entering the pitch for the launch of the Ford Cargo truck, Imagination was a rank outsider. Its bold proposal to effectively reconstruct the lake-side venue in Montreux won the pitch, but the company, fourteen strong at the time, was then left with the problem of how to deliver it. As Gary Withers observes, 'The driver of Imagination's growth hasn't really been the Imagination business, it's been our clients, because they have always pushed us. Phone rings: "Yes, you can do the Ford Cargo launch." Whoops. Fourteen people, how the hell do you deliver?' Apicella remembers that, 'the client had faith in Imagination to come up with something different each time, different and better. And there was a quantum difference, it seemed to me, in every project that happened at the time: the next one had to be better than the one before.'

Charged with the responsibility to make sure that each project was better than the last, Apicella again encountered the pressure inherent in delivering a creative solution, quickly, to the highest quality. 'I had a lot of rows with the production managers because it was my job to design the most amazing thing and it was their job to deliver it, and the two would apparently seem to contradict each other,' he recalls. 'But once we'd done a couple and everyone, including production, was so proud of having delivered them, there came a time where they would feel that I wasn't doing something extraordinary unless we had had a proper argument, because I wasn't challenging them enough.'

The spirit of constant improvement is infectious, and the designers themselves, Apicella remembers, felt the need to break new ground on a personal, as much as a company level: 'The atmosphere at the time was very dedicated; there was a certain amount of competitiveness among the designers to excel at what they were doing. Nothing was routine. Everything was an opportunity to create something that would make a mark. People worked all sorts of hours and didn't begrudge it. Perhaps it's something to do with age, but you chose to work those sort of hours not because anyone was making you, but because you chose to get it right. You could have chosen to work fewer hours and got it less right. The atmosphere was one where you simply had to excel, and it was a great atmosphere.'

Although the process is demanding, Apicella suggests, it has its own rewards. 'The need to resolve something before someone's going to make it tomorrow morning is actually very stimulating; you don't amble through the project, you race through the project, and that energy can be very creative. The thing that I remember most about Imagination was this incredibly positive, "can-do" culture – if you could imagine it, and you could explain it, then you could build it, and that's what we did. People gave much more of themselves because they weren't going to be able to find that anywhere else. There aren't many other places that work that way.'

Below, Ford's stand at the 1993 Geneva Motor Show. Designed by Lorenzo Apicella, the glass and steel sections of the stand were largely constructed off-site and delivered pre-assembled to the venue.

Inspire

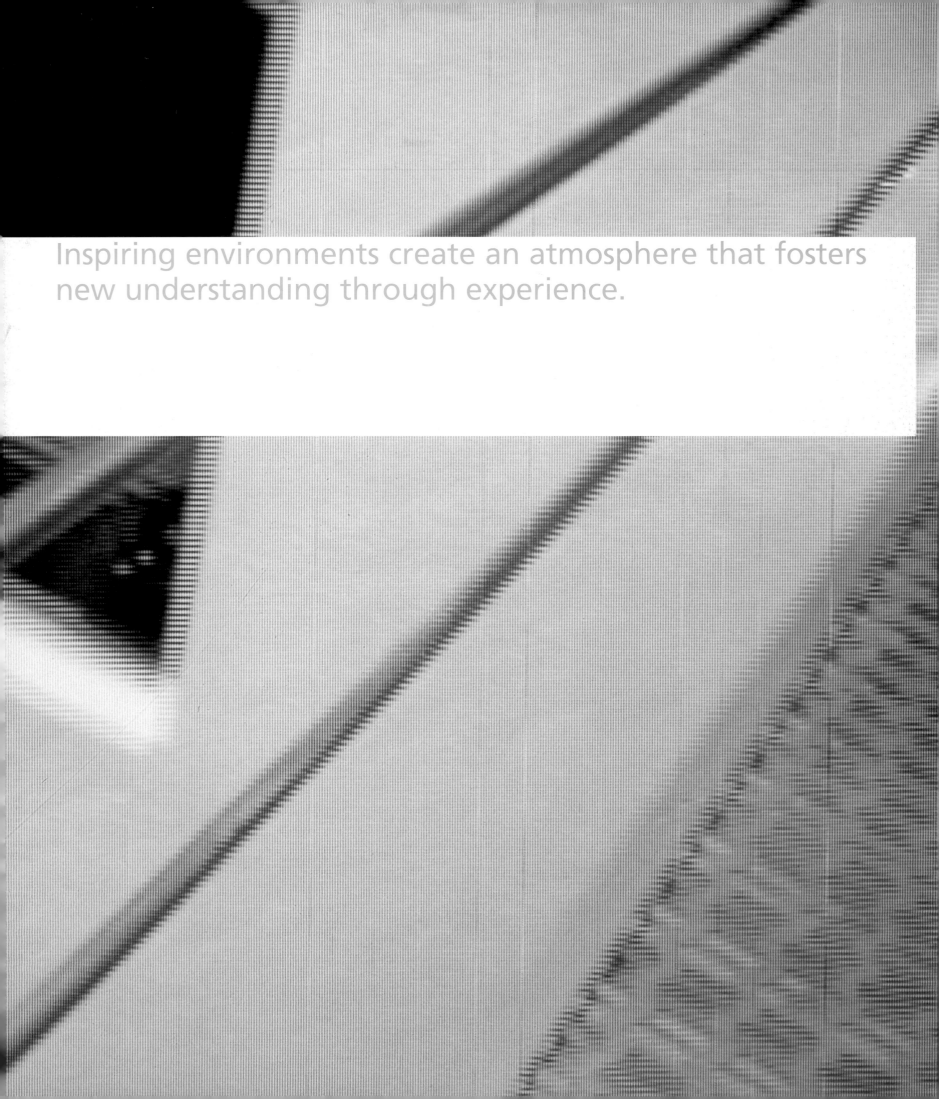

Inspiring environments create an atmosphere that fosters new understanding through experience.

Lloyd's Tercentenary Illuminations, London, 1989

A permanent architectural lighting scheme designed on the occasion of the 300th anniversary of Lloyd's of London.

Lloyd's of London's move to a modern purpose-built office in the City of London eloquently demonstrated just how far the world's oldest insurance underwriting market had come since its foundation in a London coffee house three centuries earlier. Although it generated some controversy at the time of its opening, the Richard Rogers-designed building was acclaimed as an outstanding example of high-tech architecture and soon became one of the City's best known landmarks. Three years later, when Imagination was asked to develop proposals for celebratory events to mark Lloyd's 300th anniversary, thoughts turned immediately to Lloyd's most recognizable asset. Imagination proposed a theatrically inspired architectural lighting scheme that would remain in place throughout 1989, the tercentenary year. In the event, the Council of Lloyd's was so taken with the scheme that it was developed as a permanent feature. The Lloyd's Building was Imagination's first permanent architectural lighting commission. It was quite a way for the company to cut its teeth: not only was the building a prominent landmark, but the planned scheme was, at the time, the most extensive external lighting scheme in Europe.

Although Imagination had never before lit a building, the company had a significant track record in theatrical lighting, and brought many of the techniques of the stage to bear on the building. Architectural lighting conventionally attempts to preserve the character of buildings by bathing them in a uniform light coverage. Imagination, however, attempted to emphasize different parts of the structure through a dramatic contrast of light and shade. The designers' approach was intuitive: if it looked right, it was right. In order to gauge what looked right, the designers experimented on models before installing a test scheme at the building for fine tuning. The scheme is characterized by colour, at the time used sparingly, if at all, in architectural lighting. Blue light enhances glass and stainless steel. The barrel vault atrium is lit in a warm amber colour to symbolize internal energy. External stainless steel pipework is highlighted in white using searchlights; beamed onto the building at tight angles, the searchlights accentuate the building's height. Significant technical expertise was required to put the scheme into effect: thirteen different types of fitting were used, from 1 kilowatt searchlights to 80 watt bulkhead lamps – 482 separate fittings in all. Many of the lamps and fittings were adapted especially for the project. The large horizontal pipes at the side of the building are lit with marine searchlights, which Imagination adapted by increasing their power and swapping brass housings for chrome to fit in with the building. High-pressure discharge lamps provide the blue light (the bulbs were sourced from the US as none were available in Europe) while the amber light on the barrel vault comes from high-pressure sodium lamps designed for ships' bulkheads, adapted to contain 150 watt mercury lights instead of standard bulbs. They were positioned to shine upwards from the roof terrace – for the benefit of passing air traffic – and down from the tops of the service pods at the four corners of the building. More mercury lights shine out from the inside of the atrium while white spotlights line the arch of the atrium, 'crowning' the building.

Illumination ceremony

A theatrical lighting scheme merits a theatrical illumination ceremony. Guests congregated around the atrium on various levels, while the Queen Mother pushed a button to trigger the illumination sequence. Immediately the atrium filled with a thick cloud of smoke, through which descended a 10 by 18 m (33 by 59 ft) formation of eight projection screens, suspended from a truss 49 m (160 ft) up in the atrium. The screens stopped in line with projection equipment stationed on the first and third levels. Onto the screens was projected a film describing Lloyd's history intermingled with a live feed showing the action outside the building, which culminated in a rooftop firework display that began as the building was illuminated for the first time. A hundred 18 mm candles, a hundred 12 mm candles and four seven-pound aluminium candles were detonated, ensuring that every one of the show's 45 seconds felt like its climax. The entire sequence, planned with second-by-second, inch-by-inch precision, lasted three minutes and one second, and was seen not only by guests within the building, but also by crowds outside and a television audience.

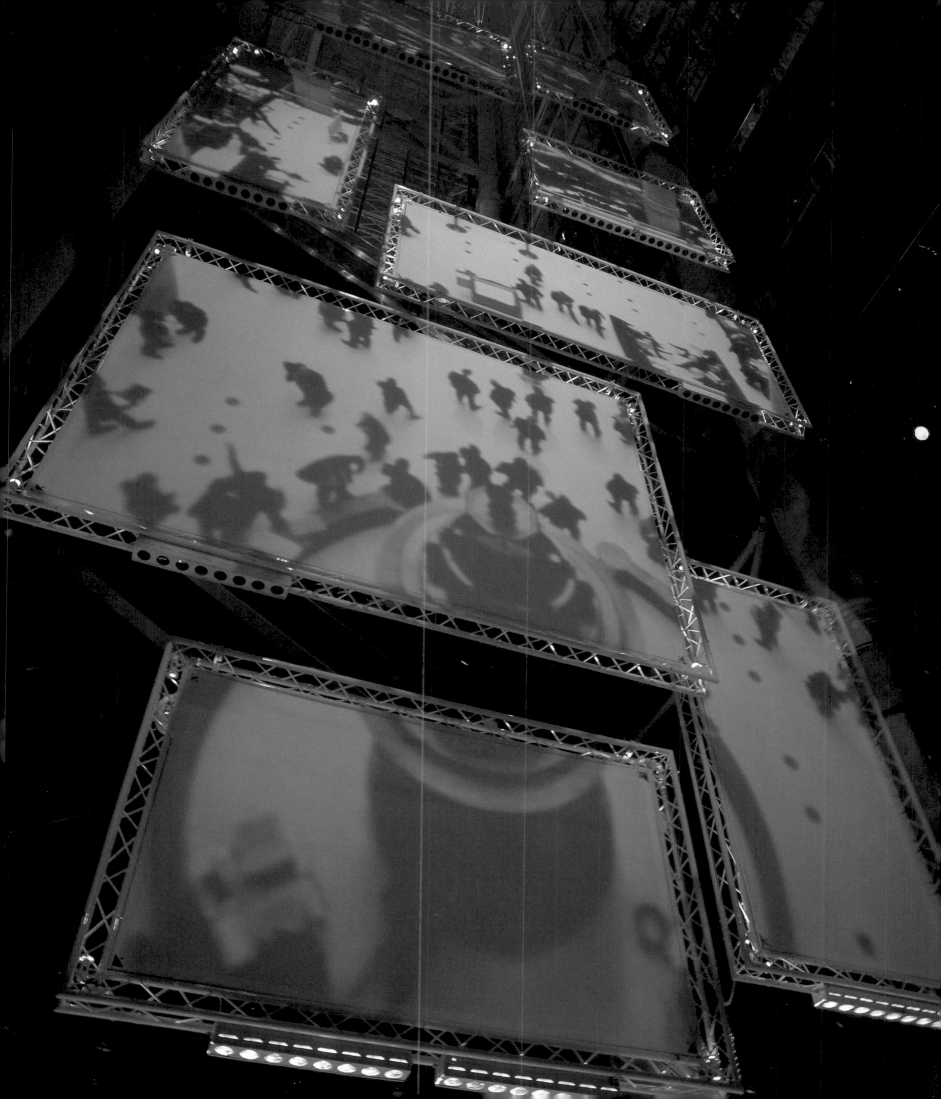

The Aurora Centre, Berlin, 1998
The conversion of a disused manufacturing complex into the temporary home of the Ford brand.

Project Aurora, a programme of activity designed to communicate to its European dealer body the ways in which 'new Ford' was adapting to meet the changing needs of its customers, was the first step in bringing about a lasting change in those customers' perceptions of the Ford brand. Developed by Imagination, the initiative grew out of a pitch to design and produce an event for dealers to be held at a conference venue in Berlin. Ford's brief had stressed that the event should both inform the dealers about the rationale behind 'new Ford' and motivate them to implement the necessary changes in their own markets. Imagination responded to the brief with an ambitious plan: instead of the single event, the company proposed Project Aurora, a twenty-four-month programme of activity. Furthermore, Imagination argued, the Berlin event itself should not be held at a regular conference venue, but should be housed in a purpose-built environment, in which delegates could experience the Ford brand for a day. Imagination had already identified a suitable site on the banks of the River Spree – a 25,000 sq m (269,000 sq ft) disused AEG electronics factory, originally designed by Peter Behrens. For six weeks in the summer of 1998 it became the Aurora Centre, the ultimate expression of the vision and character of the Ford brand – a physical manifestation of the messages of Project Aurora.

Over 20,000 Ford dealers, employees, suppliers, key clients and journalists from nineteen countries visited the Aurora Centre during its short lifetime. Every day, a group of up to 650 delegates was transported from their hotel to the centre by riverboat. Rounding a final bend in the river they saw a bridge rising from the riverbank to a dark portal in the centre of a 2,000 sq m (21,500 sq ft) graphic wall. Once inside, they were immediately immersed in a walk-through experience in which film, lighting, sound and projections evoked the increasing pace of contemporary life. They emerged into a 650-seat auditorium, where a series of presentations from Ford executives described the four key values Ford ascribed to its brand: design and package, driving dynamics, ingenuity and accessibility. As the presentations ended, two new cars, the Focus and the Cougar, were driven into the auditorium from beneath the banked seating. Following this action, the walls surrounding the auditorium drew back to reveal the scale of the Aurora Centre. Delegates made their way through four Brand DNA areas, in which the themes were developed using multimedia interactives, film, graphic displays, product demonstrations and live presentation. Visitors were able to test-drive the Focus and the Cougar on a 1.5 km (0.9 mile) asphalt test track laid around the centre. The AEG factory had been derelict for several years before the event.

Its conversion into the temporary home of the Ford brand required not only a complete refurbishment of what would become the public areas – including toilets and a restaurant – but also the construction of back-room facilities including offices, meeting rooms and kitchens. Within days of the end of the event, all additions to the site, from the 10,000 sq m (107,600 sq ft) test track to the air-conditioning, had been removed, and the site restored to its owners in its original state.

Facing page, the Aurora Centre on the bank of the River Spree.

84

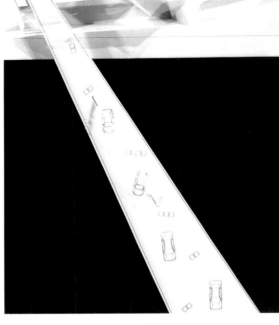

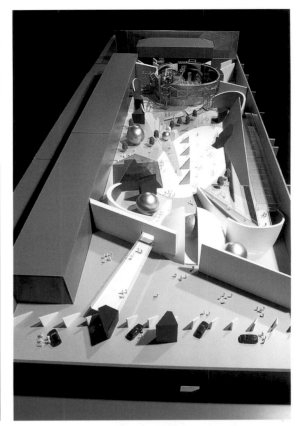

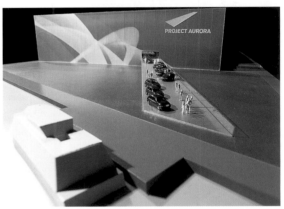

Above, concept sketch made on photographs and early models showing the bridge entrance to the Aurora Centre. Right, the bridge and facade by night.

Logistics

The Aurora Centre made significant demands on Imagination's production management and logistics teams. Quite apart from the construction of the venue itself – which took 431 people 216,000 hours – the event co-ordinators had to move hundreds of tons of equipment from London to Berlin in a fleet of 190 12 m (45 ft) trucks, book flights and hotel accommodation for 20,000 people, and hire and train staff speaking sixteen different languages. Lunch alone represented a considerable logistical challenge: over the six weeks, visitors' consumption included 143,000 bread rolls, 18 tons of broccoli, 19,000 steaks, 10,000 chicken breasts and 250,000 cups of coffee.

Above, a 1.5 km (0.9 mile) asphalt test track was laid around the centre on which visitors could test-drive the new models unveiled at the event.

Above, left to right, the walk-through experience visitors passed through on first entering the building; stills from the film shown there; the auditorium. Below, the Brand DNA areas. Imagination's angular architecture drew its inspiration from the design of Ford's cars.

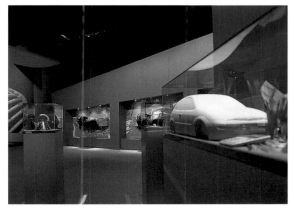

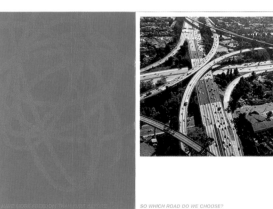

SO WHICH ROAD DO WE CHOOSE?

CONNECTIONS
PRACTICAL NEEDS WITH PERSONAL ASPIRATIONS
PLEASURE WITH RESPONSIBILITIES
DIFFERENT VALUES WITH CHANGING REALITIES
PAST SUCCESS WITH GREATER ACHIEVEMENT
WITH PEOPLE AND WITHIN OURSELVES

LIFE IS WHAT WE MAKE IT

Identity

The identity created for Project Aurora lent a visible unity to the disparate elements of a communications programme spanning two years. The 65 m (213 ft), 80-ton bridge, for example, not only dominated the facade of the Aurora Centre, but was also the main identifying feature of Ford's European motor show stands throughout the period.

Top, reading area on a revolve at the Geneva Motor Show. Bottom, visitors' brochure, designed for the Geneva Motor Show.

Below left, a listening post in the Aurora Centre allowed visitors to hear engine noises from the new Ford models, represented by the sound wave on the graphic panel behind. Right, and below right, the Birmingham and Geneva Motor Show stands took on aspects of the Aurora identity, including the colour scheme and iconic bridge. Bottom, graphic display in a Brand DNA area at the Aurora Centre.

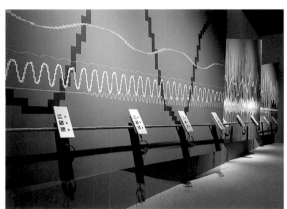

The Imagination Building, London, 1985–9

Designs for a flexible working space that represents the character and energy of Imagination.

Described by Norman Foster as 'One of the most interesting places I have seen for a long time ... a magical and joyful world hidden away behind a very ordinary facade,' the Imagination Building is an architectural landmark. Its distinctive form has become inextricably linked with the name Imagination, and in its scale, ingenuity and capacity to inspire, it is the most striking visual manifestation of the company's identity. The building, however, is not so much a monument to Imagination as the stage upon which it performs; it is the backdrop to pitches, presentations and exhibitions, the set for films, the venue for parties. It was created by Ron Herron, one of the co-founders of Archigram, the architectural collective whose ideas about instant cities and throwaway architecture had revolutionized the discipline in the early 1960s. Between 1985 and 1988 his practice, Herron Associates, had worked with Gary Withers on five schemes for Imagination at sites across London, ranging from disused warehouses in the then undeveloped Docklands to a dilapidated office block in the heart of the West End. All were characterized by what Herron referred to as 'tuning' – a blend of new and existing structures with the in-built facility to change or adapt the environment for short periods of time. Herron's interest in temporary spaces and fondness for fantastic solutions was matched by Gary Withers', and by the time the building was completed in 1989, Ron Herron had merged his practice with his most sympathetic client, becoming Herron Associates at Imagination.

The Imagination Building is actually two former Edwardian school buildings, linked by an undulating, tensioned fabric roof, creating a six-storey covered well over what was once a private road. Open-plan offices on either side look out onto the white-painted atrium and the nine steel-and-aluminium bridges that span it. Sheet steel walls at either end retract to allow large objects into the space. On the top floor, directly beneath the fabric canopy, is the glass-walled Imagination Gallery, a commercial space in which the company hosts around 200 events a year. Throughout the core of the building, white walls, natural light filtering through the roof and the ambient hum of the ventilation, as well as the sheer volume of the space, combine to create a unique atmosphere that is sufficiently neutral for it to function as backdrop to a variety of situations and events. Such an original scheme presented several technical challenges; having gained special permission from the Government to install the first permanent fabric roof in Britain, the architects and engineering consultants, Buro Happold, had to conduct extensive calculations to find the

right tensile specifications for it. In addition, most of the metalwork, from the doors and windows to the bridges and roof supports, were specially designed and manufactured. Both Herron Associates and Buro Happold were early adopters of computer modelling, which helped to speed up the design and construction process, enabling Imagination to take possession of the building a year to the day after construction had begun.

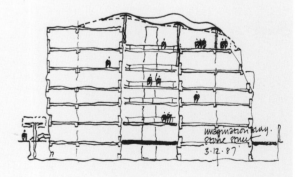

Above, sectional sketch of the Imagination Building by Ron Herron. Facing page, the interior of the Imagination Building dressed to resemble a Tokyo street for the launch of the Tokyo edition of the *Financial Times*.

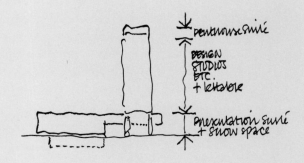

The imagination bldg.
Jan '87'

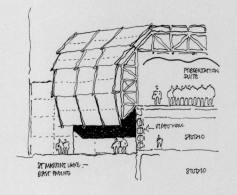

Above, sketches of a scheme for Thorn House in St Martin's Lane, central London, showing the proposed public space on the ground floor. Below, sketches of a scheme for the Marco Polo Building in Battersea, showing flexible working pods that could be configured in a variety of ways.

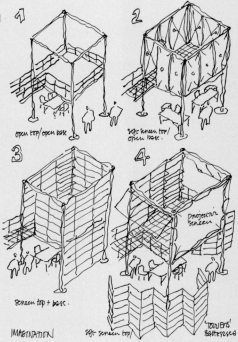

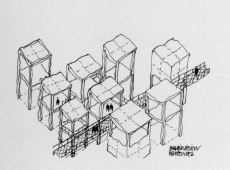

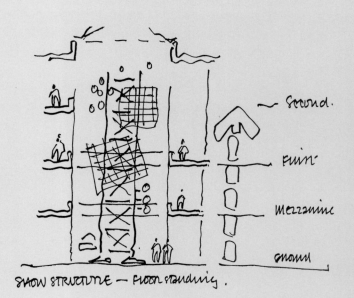

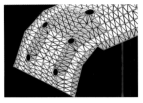
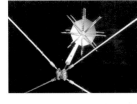

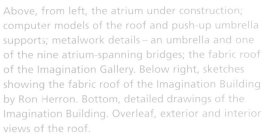

Above, from left, the atrium under construction; computer models of the roof and push-up umbrella supports; metalwork details – an umbrella and one of the nine atrium-spanning bridges; the fabric roof of the Imagination Gallery. Below right, sketches showing the fabric roof of the Imagination Building by Ron Herron. Bottom, detailed drawings of the Imagination Building. Overleaf, exterior and interior views of the roof.

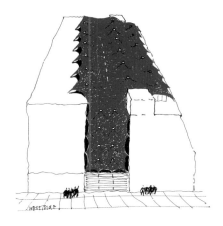

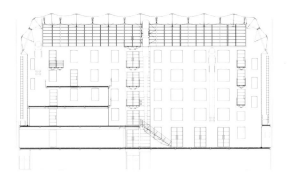

The roof

The PVC-coated polyester roof for which the building is best known was originally intended to stretch almost to ground level, but British building regulations prohibited the fabric side cladding and instead, fireproof metal walling was substituted. The undulating roof covers an area of 650 sq m (7,000 sq ft) and is supported by specially designed umbrellas, which have to be periodically adjusted to compensate for stretches in the fabric.

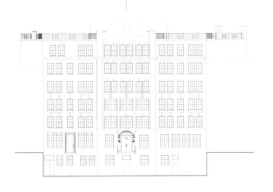

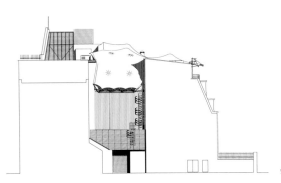

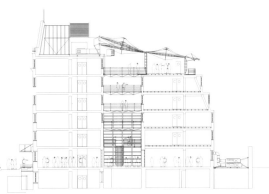

Above and below, views of the atrium. Facing page, a show for the fashion designer Julien Macdonald, featuring photographs by Sean Ellis, held in the atrium and the Imagination Gallery.

Christmas decorations

Imagination's Christmas decorations, a tradition dating back to the company's residence in Bedford Street in the late 1980s, have become something of a London institution. The outside of its offices have variously been festooned in a giant wreath, parcel wrapping and a festive table setting, all made of light. In 1999 the Store Street frontage of the building took on a traditional wintry, Christmas aspect as a forest of trees was 'planted' against a backdrop of stars. The forest consisted of thirty-four Scottish fir trees. Of these, thirty shorter firs were clustered around the base of the building, while four taller trees reached the fifth storey. Above these sat the centrepiece of the display – a star over 6 m (20 ft) in diameter. The central star was made of perforated steel, meaning that during the day, sunlight reflected off it, while at night, neon tubes shone through the hundreds of small holes. Other neon stars topped the taller trees and more were spread across the face of the building. Sixty thousand blinking fairy lights, draped over the trees, completed the display. Because of the scale of the operation, a crew of around thirty, including scaffolders, lighting designers, tree surgeons, crane drivers and caterers, worked for four days to complete the installation.

Talk, London, 1999

Visitors interacted with the pavilion and each other
in an exhibition dedicated to communication.

Talk, sponsored by BT, was the pavilion within the Millennium Dome dedicated to the ways and means of communication. BT's brief stipulated that the zone should champion better communication in the future by demonstrating that this would rely as much on individuals improving their own conversational skills as it would from being able to understand new communications technologies. Nevertheless, the zone also had to inspire people to want to try out new technologies, such as the Internet and Virtual Reality, that will affect the way we choose to transmit and receive information. It was apparent to the designers from the outset that mere representations of communication would be insufficient – visitors needed to personally experience the process of communication and all it entails, from the exchange of ideas and information to developing relationships. In this zone, form and content should be inseparable. To that end, they decided, visitors should be able to interact with one another through facilities provided by the zone, and rather than just receiving information from the exhibition, visitors should be able to feed their own views back into it. The overall experience should be one in which visitors could not only see communication realized on several levels, but would themselves be active communicators.

The starting point for the design of the exhibition was the architecture of the structure in which it would be housed. A filmed study of two people in conversation was the inspiration for two linked buildings, inclined towards each other like talking heads. Each building had a solid core over which a glass sleeve was suspended on a lattice of steel trusses, the void between the white core and the acid-etched glass panes representing the gap between people bridged by communication. Steel and glass were chosen principally for their futuristic appearance, but the difference in shape of the solid cores and glass sleeves meant that the appearance of the buildings shifted and changed depending on the angle of view. This effect was replicated through layered blocks of colour in graphic displays to visually represent a soundscape of conversation. The Dome's operator anticipated visitor flows through the zone of up to 1,800 people an hour. The nature of the zone's contents, which included popular exhibits that could only be viewed by a few people at a time, meant that the flow of people through the space had to be carefully regulated. Those waiting in the queue progressed along a rich graphic display, running the length of the two buildings, illustrating the extent to which developments in communications

technology have accelerated over the last 3,500 years. Reaching the head of the queue, visitors found themselves between the two buildings. Here, a live presenter explained what would happen on the rest of the tour with the aid of a scripted sound and lighting sequence in which the buildings literally talked to one another. On entering the ground floor of the two buildings, visitors learned about why and how we communicate as individuals. Progressing to the upper floors, they encountered some of the new technologies that will enable us to improve our talk skills in the future.

Above, early sketch showing the linked buildings. Facing page, the plinths and graphic wall on the outside of the zone told the story of developments in communications technology, and illustrated the pace of change in technological development over the last 3,500 years.

talk
talk
talk
talk
talk
talk
talk
talk
talk
talk
1800
1850
1880
1900
1920
1940
1950
1960
1970
1980

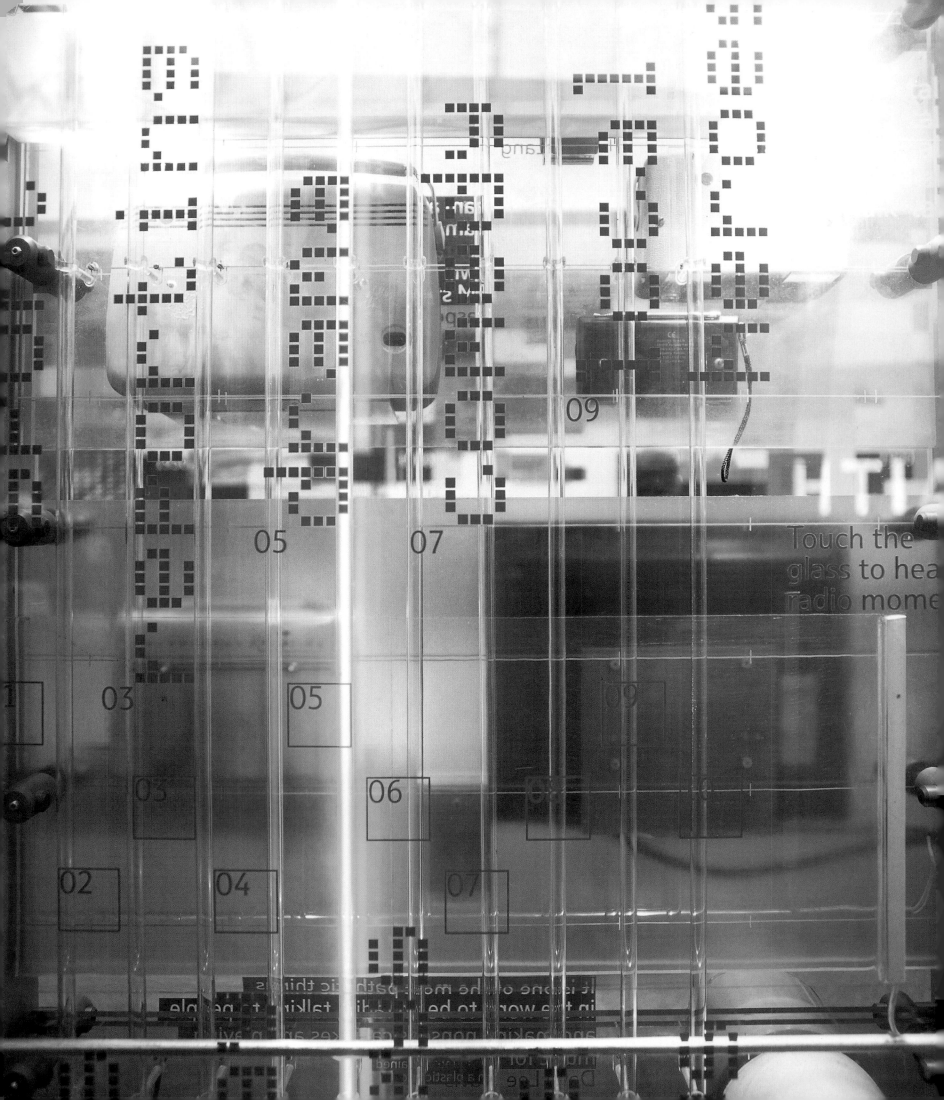

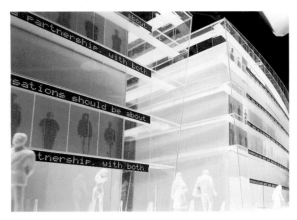

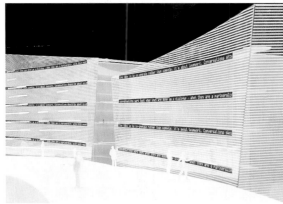

Above, early models of the zone. Lightweight and translucent materials emphasized the ephemerality of a temporary exhibition. Right, Talk viewed from the Dome's central arena and from its internal ring-road. Below and facing page, examples of the use of typography in the zone.

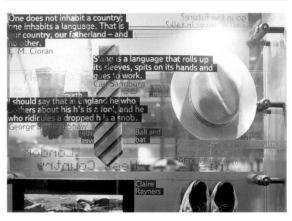

Typography

The grid within which all typographic communication was arranged derived from the proportions of the glass panels in the buildings' facades. The theme of conversation was referenced in the choice of typefaces: BT Sans was used to represent the voice of the buildings, while an LCD typeface, designed by Imagination, represented the voices of external inputs – such as the zone's visitors – into the exhibition.

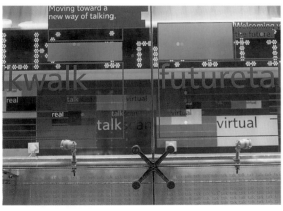

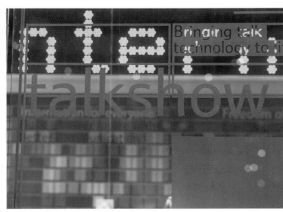

Disorientation

Entering the larger of the buildings, visitors found themselves in a darkened space in which semi-translucent projection screens were arranged around a central island. Onto these, a powerful film on the importance of communication was projected. The experience of sudden enclosure in the dark, with high noise levels and the surreal visual effect created by the layered screens apparently floating in space immediately focused visitors' attention on the message of Talk, allowing them to forget about the distractions outside in the rest of the Dome. Following the showing of the film, their disorientation was compounded by the 'talkwalk', a winding, mirrored tunnel, lined with graphic, film and animated multi-media displays demonstrating the different outcomes arising from good and bad conversations.

Above, stills from the scene-setting film shown
to visitors as they first arrived at the zone. The film
depicted instances where bad communication led to
conflict, and good communication to resolution. Below,
film, graphics and multimedia were combined in a
layered presentation in the winding 'talkwalk'.

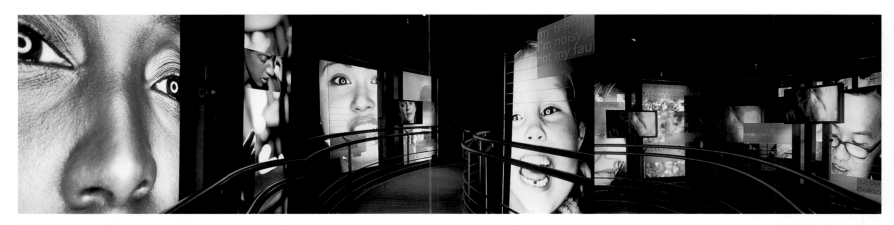

Congratulations, your mobile phone has just communicated with another object using smart technology

In the future, we will be able to control our lighting, turn on our ovens, order shopping, switch on our office alarms and access our computers – all at the touch of a button

Choose a title for your picture, enter your name and press ok

scan keyboard

we can always talk
let's always be friends
i'll be right here
you can always find me
let's stay together

select
select
select
select
select

ok

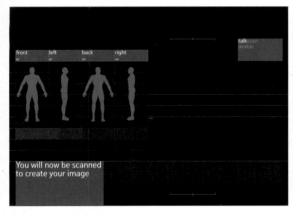

front   left   back   right

talk scan avatar

You will now be scanned to create your image

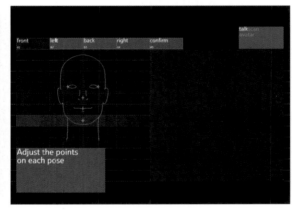

talk time leisure

In the future we will be able to take the strain from our chores and do them wherever we are

We will no longer need to go to the shops but will be able to order products from our mobile phones leaving us more time for what we really want to do

Dial 0 to continue

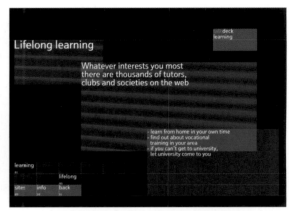

deck learning

Lifelong learning

Whatever interests you most there are thousands of tutors, clubs and societies on the web

- learn from home in your own time
- find out about vocational training in your area
- if you can't get to university, let university come to you

learning

lifelong

sites   info   back

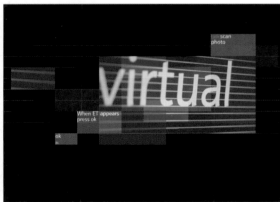

talk scan photo

virtual

When ET appears press ok

ok

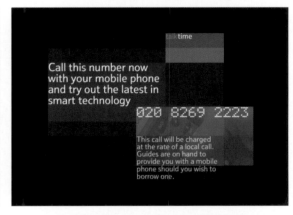

front   left   back   right   confirm

talk scan avatar

Adjust the points on each pose

talk time

Call this number now with your mobile phone and try out the latest in smart technology

020 8269 2223

This call will be charged at the rate of a local call. Guides are on hand to provide you with a mobile phone should you wish to borrow one.

Multimedia

Arriving on the first floor of the pavilion, visitors entered 'futuretalk', a three-storey high drum which physically rotated around a neon-lit central spindle. Here they were introduced for the first time to the new technology in the exhibition, through a sensory assault by interactive screens, text scrollers, LEDs and projections. Touch-screen interactives allowed visitors to input their views on communication which were then broadcast, via text scrollers on the outside of the buildings, to be viewed by the population of the Dome. Moving through the rest of the first floor, they were able to access the Internet to visit selected websites and send emails, have a three-dimensional body scan which was converted into a digital avatar and up-loaded to the web, and take part in 'talkshow', a TV studio-style discussion on the impact of technology on our communications future. Simplicity was the key with the interface design for all technology exhibits: they had to be workable by the least technically competent visitor.

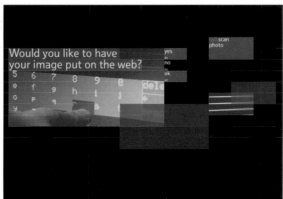

talk scan photo

Would you like to have your image put on the web?

yes
no

deck learning

Learn more Delve deeper

- be inspired
- get creative
- expand your horizons
- enjoy revision
- pass your exams
- go to the top of the class

learning

schools   uni   lifelong

back

What's so special about the internet?

deck internet

Everything you've ever wanted to know and more
- meet new friends
- see the world
- make a discovery
- play
- shop
- discuss

Look forward to surfing the web from your TV set
- mobile phone
- wristwatch
- fridge
- microwave

Touch the screen to continue

Above and left, screen-based digital interfaces for interactive exhibits in the zone including 3-D body scanners and Internet access points. Facing page, the revolving 'futuretalk' drum with neon-lit central spindle.

SPAce NK, London, 2000

Virgile & Stone aimed to create a relaxing, meditative atmosphere
in the spa and alternative treatment centre attached to the cosmetics
retailer Space NK's flagship store.

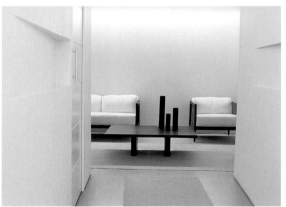

Retail Development Centre, Northampton, 1986

Built in the grounds of Castle Ashby, and linked to the stately home by a raised walkway, this Ford facility combined a show space and offices with a full-scale replica of a car dealership for the training of staff and the testing of presentation and display solutions.

Sierra Nevada '95, Spain, 1994

This concept was developed by Imagination for the promotion of the World Ski Championships. A line of inflatable yellow balloons would be laid from the sea into the Sierra Nevada mountain range, where the championships were to be held. The yellow balloons are a reference to the oranges that are the main local produce.

Futureforests.com, worldwide, 1999

The website of environmental taskforce Future Forests allows visitors to calculate how many trees they need to buy to offset the carbon emissions caused by their activities, as well as aiming to educate them about the issue of global warming through a series of easy-to-understand animations.

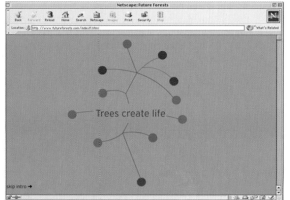
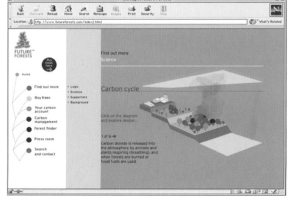

Intercraft Installation, London, 1993
A walk-through installation created for Intercraft's offices used graphics,
lighting and projections to celebrate the spirit of its new furniture range.

Nothing is ever created or destroyed

to change

Coca-Cola Lifehouse, London, 2000

Lifehouse was a three-month programme of activity in which the
need for the Coca-Cola Company to adopt a radically different approach
to consumer communications was presented to all of the company's
senior staff at events in London, Berlin and Atlanta. As the message of
the events dealt with the need to see the world through the eyes of
its consumers, it was delivered by a diverse cast of consumers in a series
of immersive environments designed to evoke their varied lifestyles.

Ford Escort and Orion Launch, Birmingham, 1990

Guests stepping into a 15,800 sq m (170,000 sq ft) black box environment, created for the launch of the new look Ford Escort and Orion within Hall 4 of the National Exhibition Centre, found themselves in a surreal world carpeted with sand. Walking over the sand, past black bulldozers ploughing back and forth through cross-lit clouds of heavy fog, they arrived at the long facade of the Ford stand, erected early for the forthcoming motor show, where the reveal of the new models was staged.

A Multi-disciplinary Company

Perspective: Mike Davies

'As technology has moved forward, and the potential has widened, you can solve problems in ways with multi-disciplinary teams that you can't solve with a single-disciplined team.'

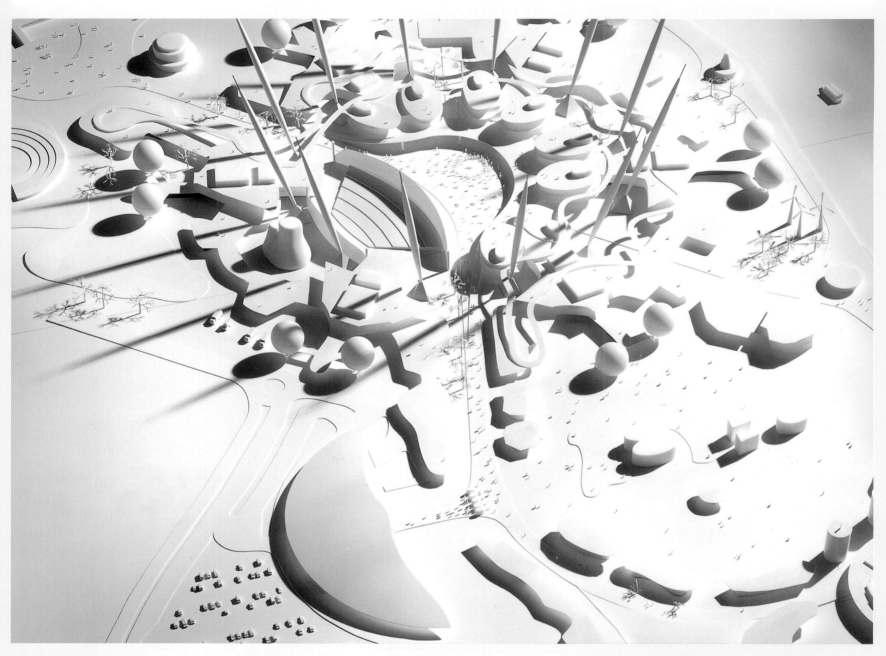

Mike Davies studied at the Architectural Association in London and UCLA in California, where he remained for some years after graduation, designing light-weight structures with the multi-disciplinary design group Chrysalis. In 1972 he joined Piano + Rogers to work on the design of the Pompidou Centre in Paris. He is a partner at the Richard Rogers Partnership and has worked on all of the company's building projects, including the Lloyd's Building, the Inmos factory and the Terminal 5 project at London's Heathrow Airport. Between 1996 and 1999, he was project director of the Millennium Dome at Greenwich, during which time he collaborated closely with Imagination.

Above, concept model showing an early configuration of buildings within and without the Millennium Dome on the Greenwich Peninsula.

When the Richard Rogers Partnership (RRP) was first asked to consider how its master plan for the Greenwich Peninsula might accommodate a proposed Millennium exhibition, partner Mike Davies drew up a list of pros and cons. Weighed against negative factors such as contamination of the site and the lack of existing infrastructure, as one of the plusses Davies listed Imagination's presence as the designer of the proposed exhibition. Critically, he believed, 'Imagination had the ability to run something that was truly multi-disciplinary.'

It was a perception based on an awareness of the company dating back to the mid-1980s, when Davies' friend Ron Herron had worked with Gary Withers on a series of schemes for the Imagination Building. In addition to favourable reports from Herron, Davies had looked to the building itself to tell him something of the character of its owner. 'The one talisman [Imagination] had was this building,' he recalls. 'If you'd gone to Pierre Chareau's Maison de Verre in Paris in the 1930s, you'd have said "Whoever built this, I want to meet." So the work testified. For this building to have been manifested required the vision of Gary and Ron, and a lot of commitment and belief, and so the building is a testament to the potential of the firm.' As much as its qualities as a breakthrough piece of architecture, however, it was what the building said about Imagination's approach to work that interested Davies. 'There are a lot of good architects who produce buildings which are about the idea of people working well together', he explains, 'and the Imagination Building is one of those. It's got all the faults and foibles of normal building fabric, but the spirit in which it is done implies that this company is about people working together rather than in separate cells.' The use of architecture to facilitate co-operative working has also been a feature of many Richard Rogers Partnership buildings, and Davies compares the Imagination Building to the Inmos Microprocessor Factory he designed in 1982, where an internal 'street' provides a central meeting place as well as allowing for circulation. 'You can't use the building without going through the central space,' explains Davies. 'What drives the building is an idea about communication and bumping into each other and sharing things. And Imagination's idea for its building was to do with that concept.'

Davies' interest in multi-disciplinary teamwork, which informed his approach to building projects such as Inmos, is long-held. His architectural thesis, written in the 1960s, took the construction of the Mount Palomar telescope – 'a project where you had a tremendously wide range of people all working in parallel across a whole range of disciplines' – as the base case for an exploration of the benefits of teamwork. In the same period, Davies and colleagues founded the multi-disciplinary Californian firm Chrysalis, and spent four years designing light-weight structures. When he began to collaborate with Imagination on what was to become the Millennium Dome in 1996, it was this multi-disciplinary aspect of the company that enthused him. 'Of all the companies we've dealt with, the ones we've enjoyed most are those that are involved in innovation, new things, looking at things from first principles, questioning, lateral thinking in synergistic groups, and Imagination is absolutely one of those,' he says.

The two companies were already working in parallel when it emerged that Imagination's proposal, for twelve separate pavilions arranged as the world's largest clock face, would be made too costly by the unique conditions of the Greenwich site. Faced with the need to trim a quarter of a billion pounds from the proposal, the two firms began to work together in earnest. From their discussions emerged the idea of a universal cover for the site, which would provide shelter, save money and allow greater flexibility for the design of the exhibition itself. The process from which the Dome emerged was, according to Davies, 'an exciting and extremely productive time' in which an apparently insurmountable challenge was resolved through creative lateral thinking.

As well as buildings, Davies' own multi-disciplinary nature has led him to design and construct a diverse array of products, from survival suits for desert environments and solar collectors to sailing craft and telescopes. And it is to this abiding enthusiasm – for astronomy and space exploration – that he looks to find an analogy for Imagination's approach to team work. 'NASA and other inter-planetary R&D teams regularly use synergistic techniques as problem-solving devices. "How do we put a 3 metre long excavating arm and analyzer in a box 15 centimetres cubed?" Nobody knows how to do it, but that's the apparently impossible task. And they assemble a team including a carpenter, a doctor, two space scientists, an engineer and an underwater oceanographer, lock them in a room and say, "Right, think about the problem." And it's an extremely powerful tool: what happens is you generate incredibly lateral ways of looking at a problem, because the carpenter has no skills in space science or mechanical engineering at all, and the doctor has even fewer.' In that instance, 'It was the carpenter who cracked it. He didn't solve the problem, but his intuitive feeling unlocked the train of thought that unlocked the problem. He said "Hold on a minute, why is this impossible? I pack a 1 metre long tape measure into this little case." And in the end what they came up with was effectively three tape measures which zipped together as they came out to form a tube, a rigid body that could reach 3 metres.' Imagination, he suggests, works in a very similar way. 'There may be some mechanical problem and somebody from the media department says, "What happens if you treated it like spooling a film?" You're using an idea from your particular area of expertise as an analogy for another one, and that cross-fertilization really works.'

The effective multi-disciplinary team, says Davies, is 'not just a lot of specialists working together, but people who can free-think across boundaries, and naturally cross territories.' In Imagination, Davies sees this happening. 'The sort of people that end up there, are employed there, coalesce there, if you like, are people with that sort of spirit,' he says. 'You don't tend to get narrow anoraks. They tend to have exposure. And just being there gives them wider exposure. They're aware of media, they're aware of advertising, they're aware of publicity, they're aware of interiors, but they might be in film.' The awareness of what is happening in other disciplines within the building, he suggests, not only allows Imagination's designers to contribute to things that are outside their own immediate area of expertise, but feeds back into their own specialisms, improving the quality of the work. It is a working method that Davies sees as being increasingly useful as the nature of the projects undertaken by companies like Imagination, or indeed the Richard Rogers Partnership, gets ever more complex. 'As technology has moved forward, and the potential has widened,' says Davies, 'you can solve problems in ways with multi-disciplinary teams that you can't solve with a single-disciplined team. So companies that have got that sort of mix, I think, have a recipe for success in an increasingly complex world.'

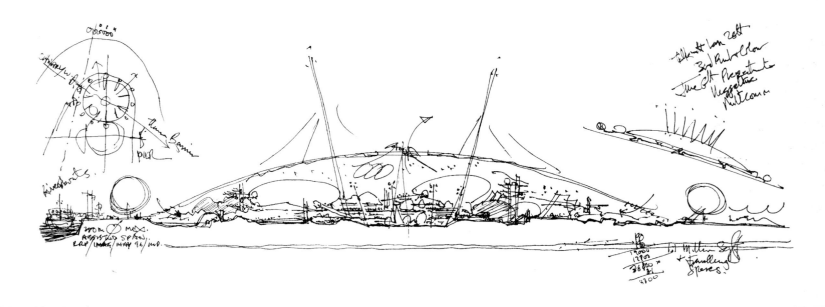

Above, early sketch of the Millennium Dome, by Mike Davies. The sketch dates from the period when Davies was collaborating closely with Imagination on plans for the exhibition on the Greenwich Peninsula.

Persuade

Persuasion is salesmanship; identifying a consumer's need for a product and building on it to stimulate desire.

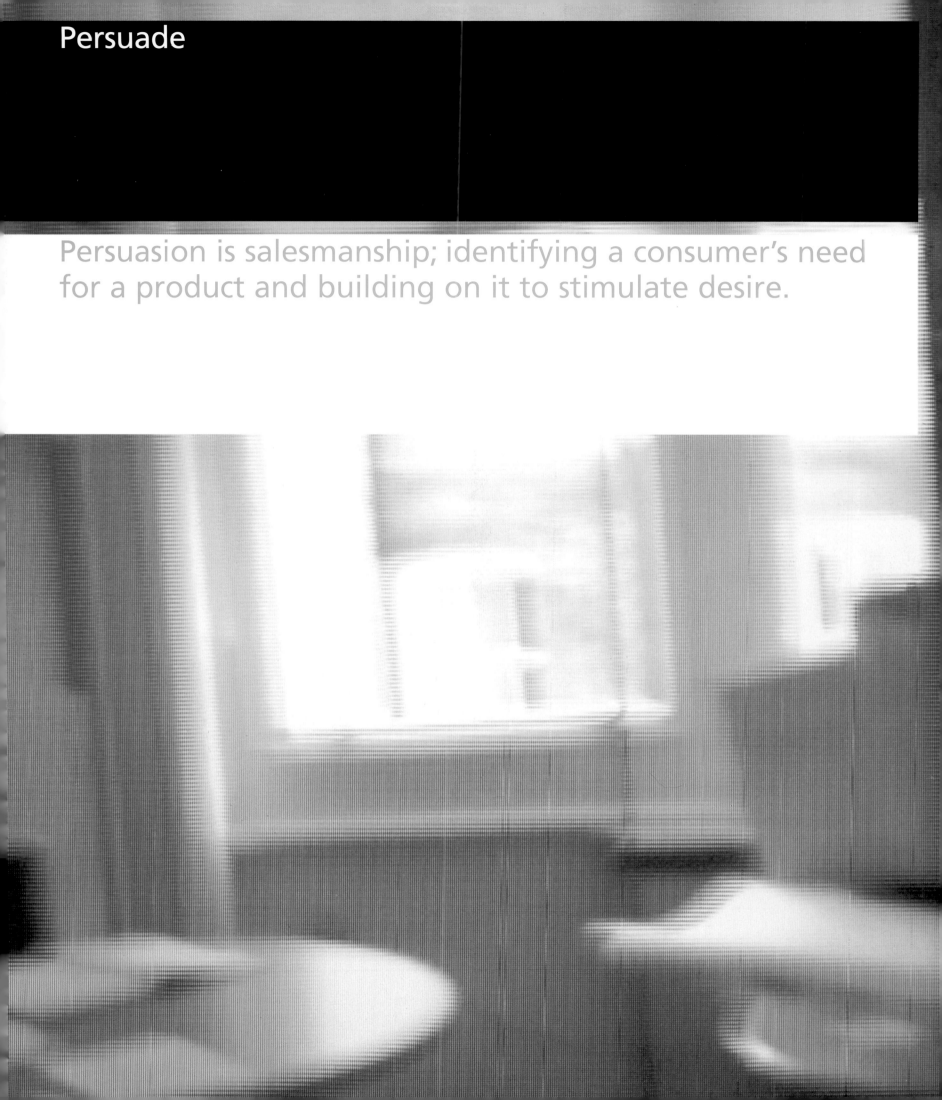

Graduate Recruitment Vehicle, UK, 1998

A touring facility that visits all of the UK's main
university campuses aiming to attract graduate recruits
to Andersen Consulting.

The paradox of graduate recruitment is that the more
prestigious the firm or industry, the more fierce the
competition for suitable graduates. The management
consultancy firm Andersen Consulting (now Accenture)
recognized that it needed a truly compelling expression
of its character and the opportunities provided by a
career in management consultancy if it was to attract
the number of top flight graduates it seeks every year.
It commissioned Virgile & Stone, which at the time was
designing the interior of its corporate HQ in London,
to devise a touring facility that would enable potential
graduate recruits at all of the UK's main University
campuses to experience for themselves the world
of management consultancy and the character of
Andersen Consulting. Graduates visiting the facility
should be able to tell not only whether the careers
offered by management consultancy are attractive
to them, but also whether they have the skills and
qualities sought by Andersen Consulting.

Virgile & Stone's designers worked with Cosby, a firm
specializing in customized trailers, to adapt the chassis
and transmission of a standard 14 m (46 ft) Daf
articulated truck into a flexible touring environment.
On arrival at each location, the truck can be assembled
and prepared for use by two people in four hours.
Using hydraulics, the sides of the vehicle are extended
outward, creating an interior floor space of

85 sq m (915 sq ft). Entry to the vehicle is via a
ramp of satin stainless steel and extruded aluminium
grille. A structural post at the corner of the ramp
supports a tensioned semi-translucent fabric canopy.
Everything needed for the assembly and operation
of the vehicle, including the ramp, furniture, and
presentation equipment is contained within it, safely
stowed during transit in specially designed fastenings
behind the graphic display panels. The interior of the
truck can be configured for several different modes
of operation. Configured for maximum capacity,
visitors enter to find a bar, reception area, cloakroom
and meeting area with a plasma screen backdrop
where up to fifty people at a time can attend lectures.
Alternatively, small groups of two or three can gather
around small tables that pull out from the wall.
In a third configuration, students can test their own
aptitude for management consultancy by taking
part in a series of interactive tests on touch-sensitive
plasma screens mounted in the walls, using software
written for the purpose by Imagination.

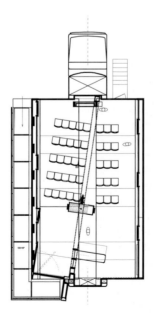
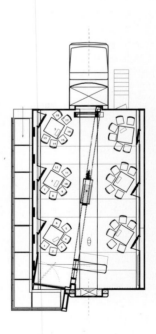
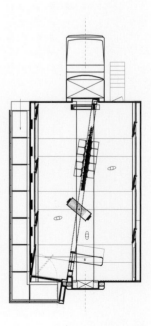

Facing page, plans showing the truck's three different modes of operation. Right, wireframe drawing showing the truck's extending sides. Far right and below, the truck in operation. The side of the vehicle and interior panels use photography by Paul Wesley Griggs.

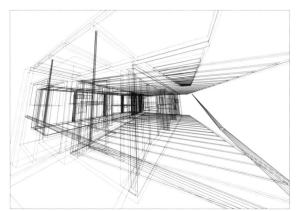

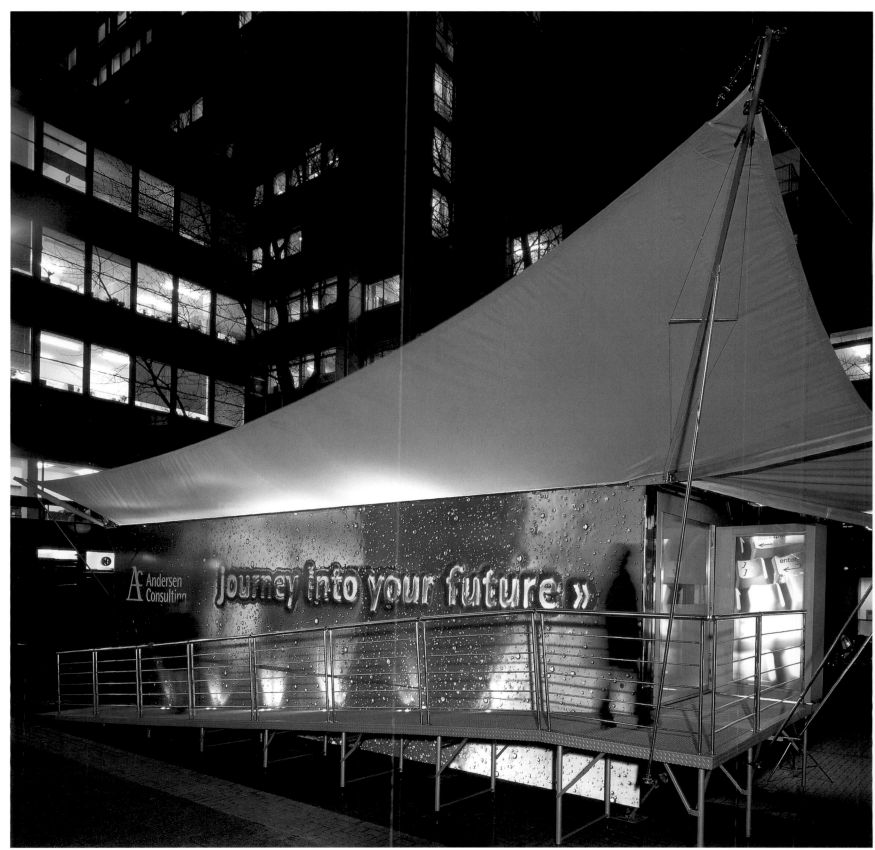

Global Autoshow Program, Detroit, 1999

Environmental design enabling the consistent presentation
of the Ford Motor Company's portfolio of marques across
the world's major motor markets.

In 1998, the Ford Motor Company decided for the first time to exhibit all of its brands together at each of the ten most important motor shows around the world. Imagination was briefed to design a physical framework to demonstrate the cohesion of the company's portfolio which could be adapted for each of the ten shows in markets across the USA, Europe and the Far East. The first show in what was called the Global Autoshow Program was the North American International Auto Show in Detroit, for which Imagination was also commissioned to design areas communicating the values of each of the Ford Motor Company's marques: Aston Martin, Jaguar, Lincoln, Mercury, Mazda and Ford (Volvo and Land Rover were added in successive years). The most basic objective of exhibiting the brands together was to dominate the Detroit show through scale and impact. Beyond this, though, the design of the stand had to demonstrate that each brand within the portfolio had a specific target market, while giving meaning and substance to the Trustmark – the umbrella identity of Ford Motor Company's whole portfolio.

A 120 m (300 ft) steel bridge spanned the site, under which each of the marques were separately presented. Arriving at the stand, the visitor would be directed up a set of escalators and onto the Trustmark bridge, from which they could look down onto the brand areas, getting a sense of the portfolio as a whole. The bridge led into the Trustmark auditorium, a 400-seat theatre, in which they could stop to watch a series of short films on subjects such as vehicle safety, which Ford Motor Company felt were equally applicable to each of its Trustmark brands. Alternatively, they could proceed directly to the ground level to navigate their way through the six architecturally distinct brand areas patchworked across a 9,500 sq m (100,000 sq ft) space. The architecture and communications materials in each of the six environments were designed to distinguish and intensify the experience of each brand. Having visually described the typical customer of each marque in a series of mood boards, the designers drew on source material as diverse as architecture, fashion and product design to create environments that did not so much resemble the brands or their customers but exude the essence of them. For the Detroit show, Imagination had partnered with the US firm ExhibitWorks, which project-managed and built the stand. With just seven weeks allowed for construction on-site, however, the designers were obliged to use materials and techniques that lent themselves to pre-fabrication of the base parts. The travertine stone floor of the Aston Martin area, for example, was not only cut into 2.4 by 1.2 m (8 by 4 ft) blocks but was also pre-built and proofed off-site to check that fit and

finish were right. Working in this way, the pieces of the stand were built over a four-month period by, at peak, over 250 joiners, steelworkers, stone cutters, leather cutters and assorted other craftsmen. Despite the fact that the stand had to be prefabricated for easy assembly, and that the show lasted just ten days, the stand and its large-scale components, such as the 62-tonne bridge, had to satisfy the same stringent weight-loading, fire and safety regulations normally applied to free-standing fixed facilities.

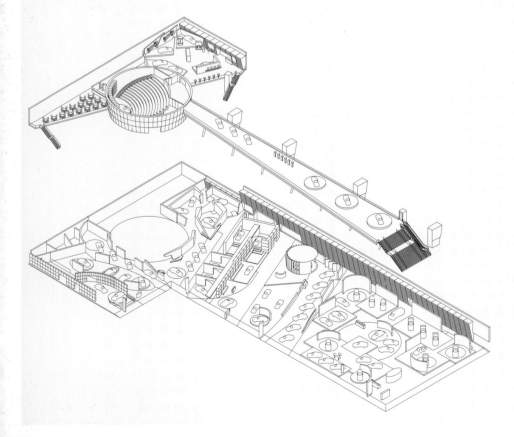

Left, axonometric diagram of the Trustmark stand, on which over seventy cars were displayed.
Facing page, view through the Lincoln brand area.

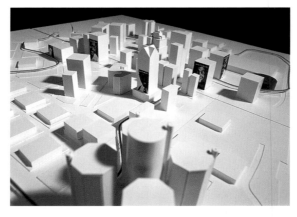

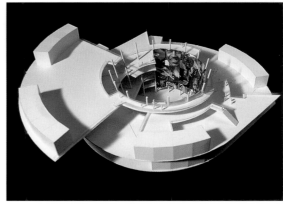

Early concept
Imagination's original concept for the Trustmark stand was to locate it in a sports arena next door to the motor show venue. The arena is served by the People Mover, an elevated monorail, and Imagination proposed to begin the visitors' experience before they arrived at the stand itself by branding the buildings en route.

Far left, the blue line on this model of Detroit represents the monorail route to Imagination's orig nal choice of venue (right).

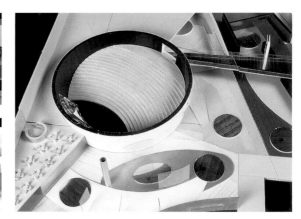

Above, models showing the bridge and auditorium. Left and below, the interior and exterior of the auditorium.

Below, clockwise from top left, the six brand areas – Lincoln, Ford, Mercury, Aston Martin, Jaguar and Mazda. Bottom, stills from the six Trustmark films shown in the auditorium.

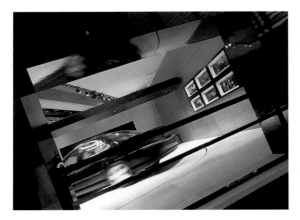

Auditorium
The Trustmark entity acted as host for the stand, and information on Ford Motor Company as a whole was given on the bridge and through presentations in the Trustmark auditorium. Here, six three-minute films covered issues such as vehicle safety and the environment, felt by Ford Motor Company to be equally applicable to each of its brands.

Above, view of the Mazda brand area from beneath
the Trustmark bridge. Facing page, view of the Lincoln
brand area from beneath the bridge.

Ericsson Brand Experience, worldwide, 1996–2000

A strategic and creative approach to define the expression of Ericsson's brand through face-to-face communication.

In 1996, Imagination was commissioned to design an exhibition stand for Ericsson's consumer products at CeBIT, the telecoms trade fair. It was the first physical manifestation of an attempt to shift the telecommunications industry's perception of Ericsson from that of a corporate multi-national communications supplier to a customer-orientated mobile communications brand name. The stand was named 'Life'. With its clean, contemporary design and use of diverse media, from postcards and brochures to music and video – not to mention a resident troupe of acrobats – it marked a significant departure for Ericsson. But more importantly, it effectively became the blueprint for a strategic and creative approach to face-to-face communications, whether in conferences, exhibitions or events, that has since been applied to all of Ericsson's live communications activities around the world.

The design principles were established to express a set of values ascribed by Imagination to the Ericsson brand. These ranged from the literal – 'straightforward communication', 'simplicity', 'warm and human', 'Scandinavian' – to the more conceptual: 'social interaction', 'entrepreneurial', 'courageous and bold', 'challenging perceptions'. These qualities underpinned every aspect of the Life stand at CeBIT '96, from the use of space, stand architecture, graphics, film and live entertainment to the tone of voice in the brand messaging and the behaviour of staff on the stand. The fundamentals established by the Life stand were refined and evolved over the following two years in conference, event and exhibition design work for Ericsson to create a clearly defined and consistent three-dimensional identity for the brand. The brand values were physically expressed in ways both general and specific: the designers aimed to create environments that were as open as possible, allowing easy access and affording a sense of welcome. The materials palette was chosen to balance man-made materials such as blue, clear or etched glass and brushed aluminium, representing Ericsson's technological background, with warmer natural materials, such as maple, beech or ash, suggesting the company's human side. But there is also a less tangible side to expressing the brand environmentally: creating an attraction to entertain the visitor, and providing hospitality to foster social interaction and create a warm, welcoming atmosphere are equally ways of communicating the Ericsson brand. Two years later, the company's stand at CeBIT '98 was designed around its advertising strapline of the time, 'Make yourself heard'. Four times an hour, screens drew down over one end of the stand, creating a darkened space in which a film was projected, depicting people from around the world talking about their thoughts, wishes, dreams and beliefs. Visitors were also encouraged to make themselves heard by using interactive exhibits to share their own hopes and dreams. Addressing such issues as visitor entertainment and the dress, attitude and behaviour of staff alongside design resulted in conferences, exhibitions and events that were not so much environments as seamless brand experiences. The experiences designed by Imagination, however, represent just a small proportion of the total: almost every day of the year, Ericsson holds an event in any one of a hundred countries around the world, ranging in size from seminars and small-scale product demonstrations to two- or three-storey stands at the world's largest trade shows. In order to ensure consistency across all of its face-to-face communications, the company asked Imagination to formalize the Ericsson brand experience principles in a set of *Events Guidelines*, published in 1999.

Facing page, a selection of the messages left by visitors to Ericsson's 'Make Yourself Heard' stand at CeBIT '98. They were encouraged to reveal their thoughts, wishes, dreams and beliefs.

I am happy when the sun is shining.
Name: Patrick
City: Stockholm
200

What makes me happy is playing with my two sons.
Name: Helen
City: Lund
201

Extreme paging.
Name: Peer, Marty und Anahid
City: Hannover
202

Mir geht es gut.
Name: Coktas
City: Duisburg
203

Daisy, wenn Du jetzt Fernsehen guckst, ruf mich jetzt an. Ich freue mich über meine Frau.
204

I dream of a big car.
Name: Dalibor
City: Prag
205

I wish to have an Ericsson mobile phone.
City: Prag
206

I want to live forever
Name: Helge
City: Düsseldorf
208

Mich macht glücklich, wenn alles ruhig ist.
Name: Valerio
City: Gifhorn
209

Ein einfacher Urlaub, alle Scheine machen mich glücklich.
Name: Alexander
City: Bingen
210

Ich freue mich über Gesundheit.
Name: Sven
City: Limberg
211

Ich wünsche mit, weiterhin so glücklich zu sein mit meiner Frau.
Name: Blankenberg
City: Wolfenbüttel
212

Ich wünsche mir, daß es endlich warm wird und Sommer
Name: Sven
City: Hannover
213

Ich habe Anika auch überzeugt, Olli - Sie findet Dich jetzt auch ganz toll.
Name: Anika und Kristine
City: Hannover
214

Josi, Du machst mich Glücklich, meine Kleine.
Name: Andreas
City: Stuttgart
215

Hi! I think CeBIT is really great stuff.
Name: Jim
City: Cincinnati
216

I want a beer please
Name: Myrin
City: Stockholm
217

Mich macht Erfolg glücklich.
Name: Marko
City: Schwäbisch-Gmünd
218

Dies ist ein ganz toller Stand.
Name: Ragnar
City: Berlin
219

Ich fühle mich ganz toll hier bei Ericcson !
Name: Jochi
City: Freiburg
220

Mich würde glücklich machen, wenn ich mein Leben lang gesund und fit bliebe.
Name: Joachim
City: Lohmar
221

I wanna go home!!!
Name: Kamps
City: Zvvammerdam
222

I would like to dance.
Name: Costas
City: Greece
223

Good friends make me happy. I am a sentimental guy.
Name: Hallstein
City: Kristiansand
224

Das neue Jahrhundert hat begonnen.
Name: Sven
City: Wörrstadt
225

Ich wünsche mir keinen starken Mann, ich wünsche mir ein starkes Auto.
Name: Edeltraud
City: Gelsenkirchen
226

Zufriedene Menschen machen mich glücklich
Name: Volker
City: Stauffenberg
227

Kerstin makes me happy.
Name: Fadi
City: Stockholm
228

My girlfriend makes me happy
Name: Claus
City: Copenhagen
229

Ich wünsche mir, daß ich Fußballstar werde.
Name: Patrick
City: Köln
230

Es macht mich glücklich mit Ericsson zu telefonieren.
Name: Heinz
City: Lüneburg
231

I wish Sunshine
Name: George
City: Suwalki
232

Geld, ein schönes Auto, ein Haus und ein Pferd machen mich glücklich.
Name: Steve
City: Bremen
233

You can't kill time without injuring eternity
Name: Paul
City: Sweden
234

To drink a nice cup of coffee with my mother in law makes me happy.
Name: Paul
City: Amsterdam
235

Handies machen mich glücklich.
Name: Jukka
City: Düsseldorf
236

I believe in trust and love and sharing responsibility.
237

Ich freue mich, wenn ich abends nach Hause komme, und meine Kinder begrüßen mich.
Name: Arno
City: Gründau
238

Was mich glücklich macht, ist, anderen Leuten zu helfen.
Name: Gianni
City: Zürich
239

Ich denke, daß die Telekommunikationsindustrie die Automobilindustrie in 10 Jahren überflügelt hat.
Name: Andreas
City: Frankfurt
240

Greetings from Finland.
Name: Marco
City: Finland
241

It would make me happy to find Norbert Luken
Name: Noah
City: London
242

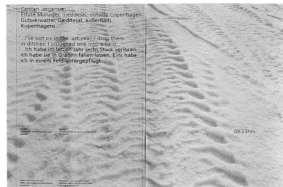

Above, acrobats perform on the Life stand at CeBIT '96. Left, cover and and spreads from the Life brochure, designed for CeBIT '96. Below, the Ericsson logo set against a blue glass wall on the Voice stand at CeBIT '97.

Attractions

Creating an attraction is an important part of the Ericsson brand experience. For the Life stand at CeBIT '96, Imagination developed a series of eight-minute performances by acrobats on a frame over a launch area for new products. As well as attracting people to the stand, the acrobats' expressive movements were intended as a metaphor for the communication Ericsson aims to facilitate between its customers. Performers were used again on the 'Voice' stand at CeBIT the following year, when they turned the stand into a constantly shifting collage of images by sliding graphic panels up and down its length.

Creating a balance

The blue glass wall against which the Ericsson logo was set was the starting point for the materials palette. Its stark, modern effect was balanced by the use of softer, natural materials such as wood, as well as the use of large-scale photographs of 'real' people in 'real' situations.

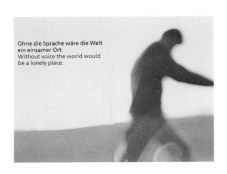

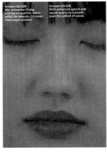

Left, cover and spreads from the *Voice* brochure, designed for CeBIT '97. Facing page, acrobats perform among the sliding graphic panels of the Voice stand at CeBIT '97.

Simplicity
Ericsson's Systems stand at CeBIT '98 was designed to communicate its intention to establish a presence in the fast-growing infocoms market. The large stand was made comprehensible to the visitor by its division into easily identifiable areas. The 'big picture' was presented in a film, *Information Revolution*, shown in a futuristic video gallery, while the remainder of the stand was divided into three zones looking at the future telecommunications needs of consumers at home, in the office and on the move.

Below, stills from the film *Information Revolution*, which was screened in the video gallery (bottom) of the Ericsson Systems stand at CeBIT '98.

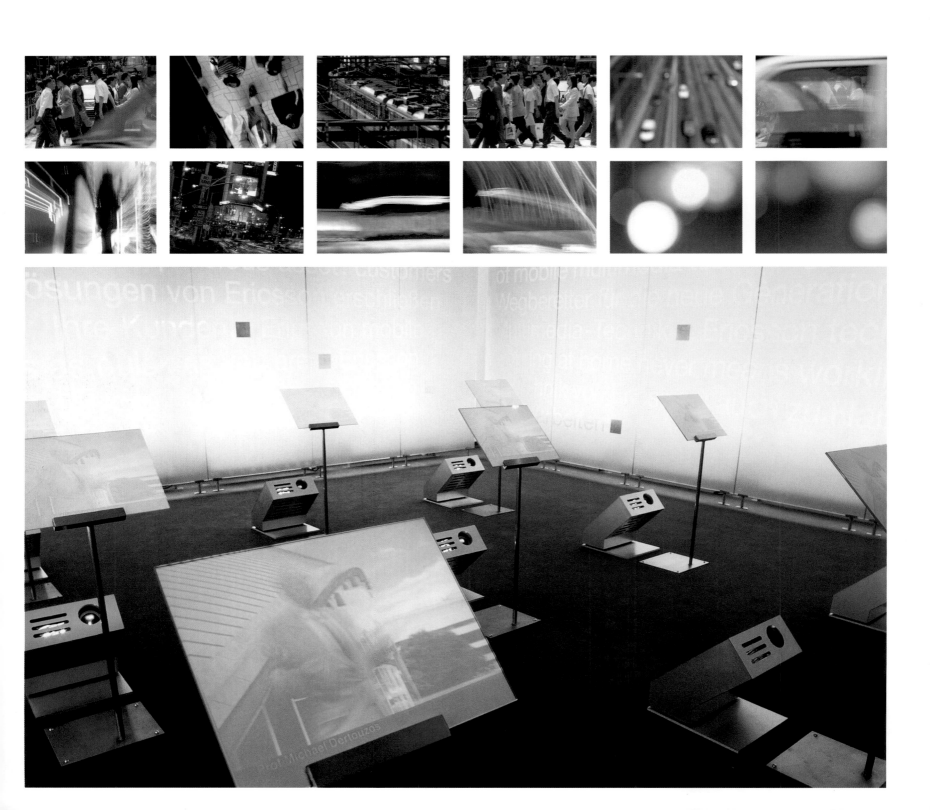

Top, the café at Ericsson's Düsseldorf offices. Above, renderings of the architectural lighting scheme and blue glass 'cap' applied to Ericsson's Düsseldorf offices. Below, the visitor centre at Ericsson's corporate headquarters in Kista, Sweden.

Communicating offices

The same brand experience principles that had been applied to its conference and exhibitions presence were applied to Ericsson's own offices in Düsseldorf, Germany, in 1998, and in a visitor centre at Kista, Sweden, the following year. For the Düsseldorf offices, Imagination created a blue glass light box to cap the building and implemented an architectural lighting scheme for its exterior. Inside, a new café, meeting rooms and Customer Communications Centre were added to provide a warm welcome for visitors.

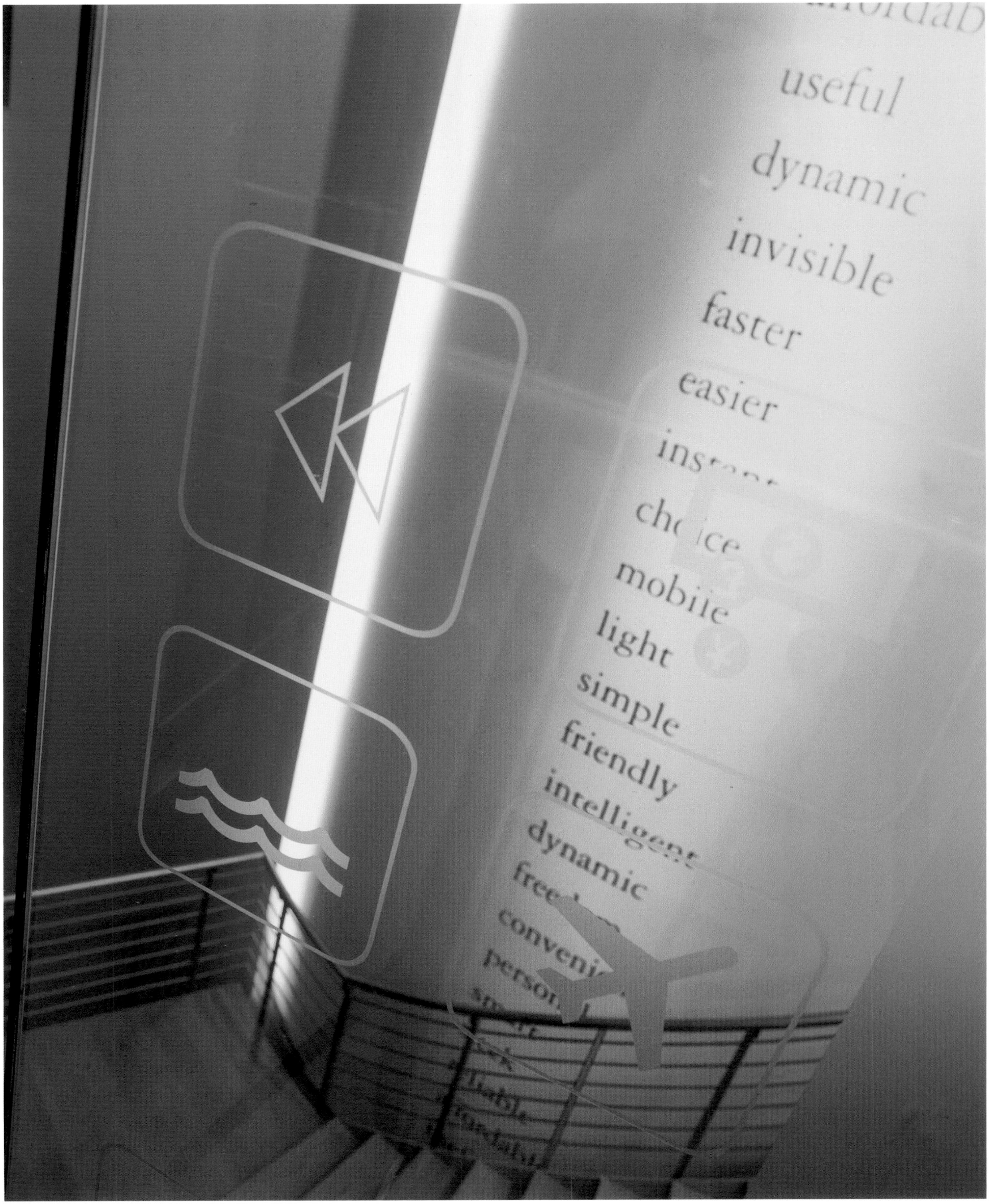

useful

dynamic

invisible

faster

easier

inst...

choice

mobile

light

simple

friendly

intelligent

dynamic

free...

conveni...

person...

Facing page and above, exhibition stand for the trade show Telecom '99 that brought to life Ericsson's vision for the mobile and Internet-orientated communications future. Below, environment and literature for wwwireless ambition.

Hospitality

'wwwireless ambition' was a three-day event hosted by Ericsson in Stockholm. Mobile phone network operators were flown from around the world to discuss emerging communications technologies and trends. The environment itself was created from a former car factory using nothing more substantial than lighting, projections and fabric. Hospitality, in the form of a culturally rich mix of entertainment and food, was provided in a Global Food Village.

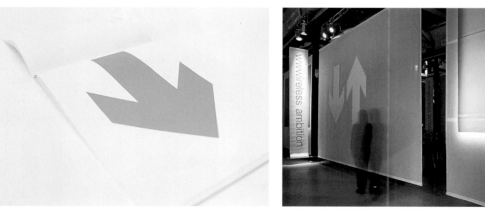

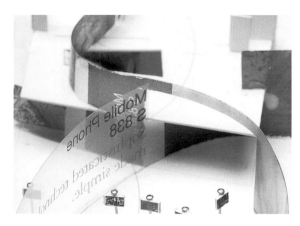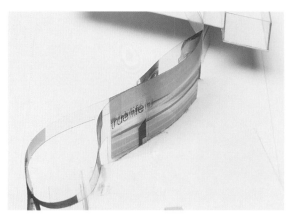

Above, sketch models of the Now Generation stand at CeBIT '99. Right and below, the Now Generation stand. Below right, four postcards designed for the stand. Bottom, stills from *Now Generation*, a film shown at CeBIT '99.

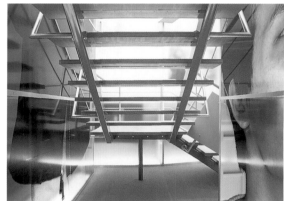

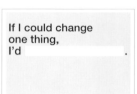

If I could change
one thing,
I'd   .

independence
freedom
changing your mind
making up the rules as you go along
no agendas, or timetables
no plans, just whims
laughing, larking, going with the flow
where next?
who knows.

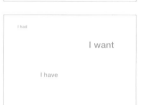

I had

            I want

I have

These are a few of my
favourite things:
1
2
3
4
5

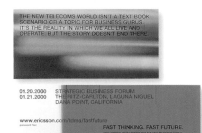

Above left, invitation and literature for Ericsson's 'Fast Thinking, Fast Future' conference. Above right, invitation to Ericsson's 'Making Sense of the New Economy' conference. Below, concept drawings of the e-cycle phone packaging and disposal bin and the Cool Sauna.

Future concepts

Imagination has developed a number of concepts which take the Ericsson brand experience outside the business-to-business communications arena, including the Cool Sauna and the disposable phone. Inherently Scandinavian, the Cool Sauna could be installed at a club, a festival or just situated within a hot urban environment. Water-resistant phones would be provided for use by people relaxing in the refrigerated micro-climate. The e-cycle phone would be designed for recycling. Made of card, with basic functionality and just twelve minutes of talktime, it would be disposed of after use in special Ericsson recycling bins.

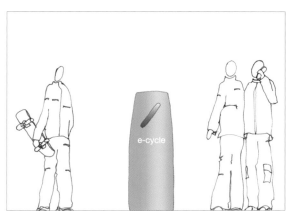

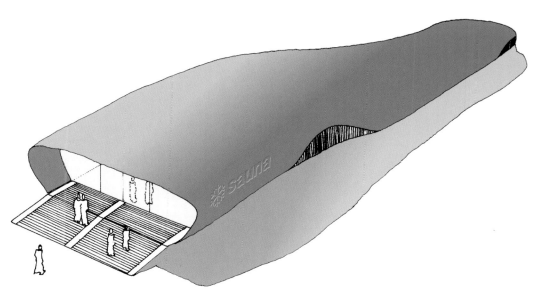

Kiss, worldwide, 2000

In a TV commercial broadcast as part of Coca-Cola's marketing programme for the Olympic Games, Imagination aimed to create a wordless piece of communication that would work around the world.

Throughout the life of the company, Imagination has been active on the peripheries of advertising, creating infomercials and designing sets for TV ads, as well as poster and print campaigns for various clients. Some of its films, made for other uses, have even been screened as commercials. But until 'Kiss', the company had never created a made-for-purpose TV commercial. The opportunity to move into this new medium came about somewhat unexpectedly, when Coca-Cola asked the company to create a commercial for use as part of its media campaign to support the Sydney Olympic Games. At the same time, Imagination was staging a day-long brand experience event for Coca-Cola. As a finale, the audience, which consisted of most of Coca-Cola's worldwide senior management, witnessed the performance by a cast of consumers of a specially written song, 'Our World'. Recognizing the impact of the song on the audience, Coca-Cola asked Imagination how this piece of music, based around contrasting harmonies to create a swelling, anthemic sound, might be given a wider audience. It was agreed that the song should be the basis of the commercial, due to air two weeks later. The decision triggered a flurry of activity in which the commercial was scripted, cast, shot, edited and distributed in fourteen days.

The perennial problem of creating communications for a multinational audience goes beyond language barriers: a lack of shared references and differing social and cultural mores combine to mean that what works in one market might well alienate viewers in other territories. In an effort to avoid such potential problems, Imagination aimed to create a commercial that as well as being wordless, depicted a scenario that was common to all the peoples of the world, emphasizing our shared humanity and chiming with the inclusive spirit of the Olympics. The concept of 'Kiss' was simple but effective: a chain of people pass a kiss from one to another. From the types of kiss the viewer can guess at the nature of the relationships between the diverse group of people seen to connect parents and children, husband and wife, friends and lovers – and the range of messages conveyed by a kiss – support, love, friendship, parental pride, joy. The characters are arranged in a line, along which the camera pans, following the progress of the kiss. The sequence begins with a woman turning away from the camera to kiss a man, and ends with the same woman, at the other end of the chain, turning back to the camera, having just watched a particularly passionate kiss. 'Our World', the song that provided the inspiration for the commercial, was itself rearranged, and recorded by Heather Small of pop group M People. The commercial was made available by Coca-Cola to all of its marketing departments, and was screened in many markets worldwide.

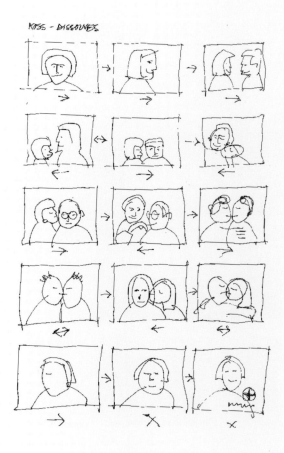

Above, concept sketch for 'Kiss'.
Facing page, stills sequence.

British Army Advertising Typography, UK, 1995

Imagination developed the bold animated typography that framed provocative questions and imparted career information in Saatchi & Saatchi's British Army recruitment advertising campaign.

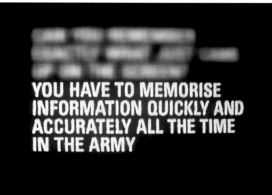

Bond.ericsson.com, worldwide, 1997

Created to promote Ericsson's sponsorship of the Bond film *Tomorrow Never Dies*, this youth-orientated website featured games, gadgets and downloadable giveaways. Visitors were guided around its attractions by the voice of James Bond's quartermaster, Q.

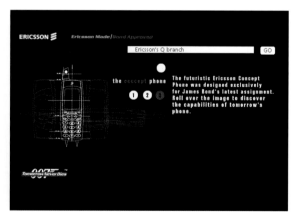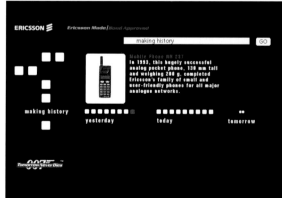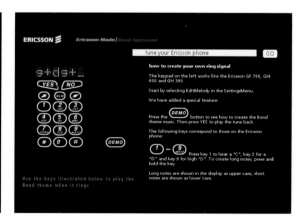

Yves Saint Laurent Store, Paris, 1998

In its Avenue Victor Hugo store for Yves Saint Laurent,
Virgile & Stone aimed to evoke the ambience of a fashion studio
of the 1960s. Specially designed large-scale benches over
which pendant lights are suspended recall the cutting tables
of a fashion atelier, while a catwalk, made of black stained
and veneered wood, was introduced as a linear architectural
element into the clean white shell of the store.

Symbian Exhibition Stand, Hanover, 1999

Symbian is the developer of operating system software for 'third-generation' mobile phones. To convey the message that it viewed the future as a voyage of discovery on which it would embark with anyone who wanted to join in, Imagination selected the theme of 'departures' for its CeBIT stand, which was designed to resemble an airport departure lounge complete with check-in desks and flight information monitors.

Visteon Exhibition Stand, Paris, 2000
Imagination's photographers created a series of reportage
images, used to add a sense of the drama and pace of life
on the road to Visteon's stand at the Paris Motor Show.

Digital Road, Birmingham, 2000

Housed in seven walk-in viewing pods on the Ford Motor Company stand at the Birmingham Motor Show, the interactive Digital Road animations presented future automotive devices that use an in-car Internet connection to facilitate services such as breakdown alerts and remote fault diagnosis. Users were able to select the one of a number of alternative scenarios which most closely resembled the way they used their own car to see when and where such services would be useful.

Land Rover Exhibition Stand, Birmingham, 2000

The architecture and choice of natural materials such as wood and leather for Land Rover's Birmingham Motor Show stand were inspired by the company's association with the great outdoors. An aviary-like cable net enclosed the space while a double-deck structure, dressed to look like a bird-watcher's hide, housed product displays and hospitality facilities.

The Extended Family

Perspective: Ian Liddell

'It's unusual to have a relationship go on like this for quite so long, but that's Imagination's way of working. Gary has his guys that he can always ring up, who he can trust will come in and deliver every time.'

A founding partner of Buro Happold, Ian Liddell CBE is a leading expert in the fast developing field of light-weight structures. As an engineer, he has worked regularly with Imagination since the late 1970s, and collaborated with the company and the Richard Rogers Partnership on the early stages of the Millennium Dome proposal, for which he later won the 1999 Royal Academy of Engineering MacRobert Award, the most prestigious prize for UK engineering.

Above, structural design detail from Talk, one of two zones in the Millennium Dome on which Imagination worked closely with its long-term engineering consultant, Buro Happold.

In its earliest days, with a full-time staff of less than ten, Imagination was reliant on a diverse collection of freelance associates to design and deliver its projects. Lighting and projections, for example, were supplied by people whose principal occupations were in the theatre or rock-and-roll productions, but who would regularly take on Imagination's conference and exhibitions work for some out-of-hours diversity. Over the following two decades, as the company grew to nearly 500-strong, specialist departments were created in areas such as lighting and projections so that today, almost every project is designed entirely in-house. But despite the scope of its expertise, Imagination is still reliant on a close network of associates, ranging from engineering consultants to steel fabricators, rigging specialists to hauliers, to physically deliver its ideas, and the company's perception of itself, not as a single entity working in isolation but as the hub of an extended network, remains true today.

Gary Withers refers to Imagination, as 'a family', albeit a large one. The suppliers and contractors that have worked with Imagination over the years are, by extension, 'the extended family'. They are numerous – 'If you were to collect all the people that have worked with us since we started,' he says, 'you'd fill the Albert Hall' – but the relationships are close and, critically, they are long-lasting. 'Buro Happold have been our structural engineers for twenty-five years,' says Withers. 'Boyden and Company are quantity surveyors who I've known for thirty years. Service Photography goes back thirty years. Sheetfabs goes back twenty years. There are people at Versatile, the scenic construction company, who I can remember being born; now they are charge hands running a crew.'

'It's what they call, in the modern parlance, "partnering",' observes Ian Liddell, a founding partner of Buro Happold, which has worked with Imagination since the the birth of both firms in the late 1970s. 'It's unusual to have a relationship go on like this for quite so long, but I think that's Imagination's way of working. Gary has his guys that he can always ring up, and they're people he likes to work with, who he can trust will come in and deliver every time.' While the fact that personal friendships have developed alongside business relationships is important, it is not the only reason for such long-term associations. The nature of Imagination's business, in which one-off, complex projects have to be undertaken usually at short notice and often under a variety of taxing circumstances, means that the level of understanding achieved between Imagination and its suppliers over time plays its own critical part in the company's ability to promise – and deliver – against the odds each time.

'As far as I'm concerned,' says Withers, 'the close family of contractors is our hidden strength. All the things we've done over the years have been through building a very good relationship with our suppliers, because without them we can't do anything.'

The need to 'do anything' is something with which Liddell has become very familiar as the two firms have collaborated on exhibitions and permanent buildings, temporary performance spaces and touring structures. The relationship began with a series of fabric pyramids for a toy fair in Birmingham, which set the pace for what was to follow. 'We were whisked off our feet, in the usual way,' he recalls. 'The deadlines that sometimes get set for projects mean that everybody's running around madly, but it's very stimulating working to very short timescales. With Imagination, it's very much: get on and get it done and get it in there for next week.' Imagination's projects may happen much quicker than the buildings that form the bulk of Buro Happold's work, but Liddell enjoys the difference. 'Gary energizes things enormously,' he explains. 'He gets everybody going, somehow; people will do things for Imagination that they would never do for anybody else. He'll say "We're going to do this display with banners 80 metres high for the Olympics." "Yes Gary."' As well as the energy, Liddell relishes the diversity of the challenges presented by Imagination, which have ranged from how to create touring exhibition spaces within blow-moulded titanium spheres to how to construct an auditorium eight storeys above the ground in BT's atrium, with no fixed supports on the surrounding walls. 'I think Gary recognizes the scale of the challenges,' says Liddell, 'but he believes that his gang can get round them. And, by and large, they do.'

That its partners will go the extra mile for a long-term and trusted client is a great advantage to Imagination, but more important, perhaps, is the better understanding brought about by familiarity. As an example, Gary Withers cites Top Telco, a 16,000 sq m (170,000 sq ft) exhibition with a levitating geodesic dome as its centrepiece, designed and built in just sixteen weeks. 'We shorthanded a lot,' remembers Withers. 'The design team were actually on-site, in Portakabins, designing it, giving sketch drawings to the contractors, and they were going out and positioning it. It was a pretty extraordinary short-cut on all the normal processes to get it done in the time.' Ian Liddell first introduced Imagination to its regular steel fabricator, Sheetfabs, and confirms the account: 'Imagination works very closely with Sheetfabs and they can just grab the drawings out of their hands and go away and detail them; they'll just take something, draw it up and build it,' he says. In his own experience, Liddell has found that the closeness of the relationship allows for a briefing shorthand that sets a clear objective, but relies on the contractor's familiarity with Imagination's priorities and working methods to fill in the missing pieces. He gives as an example a demountable frame commissioned by Imagination for use on exhibition stands. 'That was typical Imagination,' he explains. 'Gary said, 'What I want is a grid of columns and beams, which are going to be pre-wired, so you can clip in lights without seeing the cables at all. I want to go to the show situation, put out the floor structure with the cables under it, clip this kit together, and put the cars in the middle'. And that was his brief.'

Liddell's solution was an elegant piece of engineering – a secret internal connection system allowed the columns and beams to be clamped together with a simple twist – but as he explains, the mechanics of the construction are of secondary importance to his client. Gary Withers, suggests Liddell, 'is totally uncompromising in the finished effect. There are lots of things he doesn't worry about, some components can look pretty rough underneath, but the finished effect will be terrific.' The longevity of Imagination's relationship with its 'extended family' gives it confidence that not only will its partners share its desire for a 'terrific finished effect', but that they will be able to make it work in a way that is sympathetic to Imagination's creative vision.

This confidence is born out of what Withers describes as 'a great deal of mutual respect,' which gives Imagination's contractors license to query a brief when they need to, creating a truly collaborative relationship between client and supplier. Sometimes, it's just the balancing factor that's required: 'You sometimes have to do a bit of managing their expectations,' laughs Ian Liddell, 'steering them round a bit to a more reasonable way of thinking. But you get there in the end because the ideas merge, and it works.'

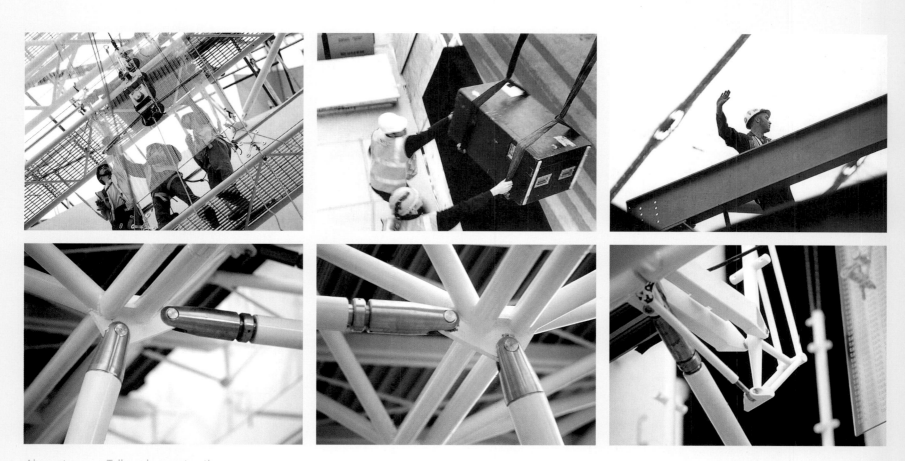

Above, top row, Talk under construction.
Above, bottom row, structural details of Talk.

Amaze

To create an unforgettable experience, the designer must understand the hopes and expectations of an audience, and then exceed them.

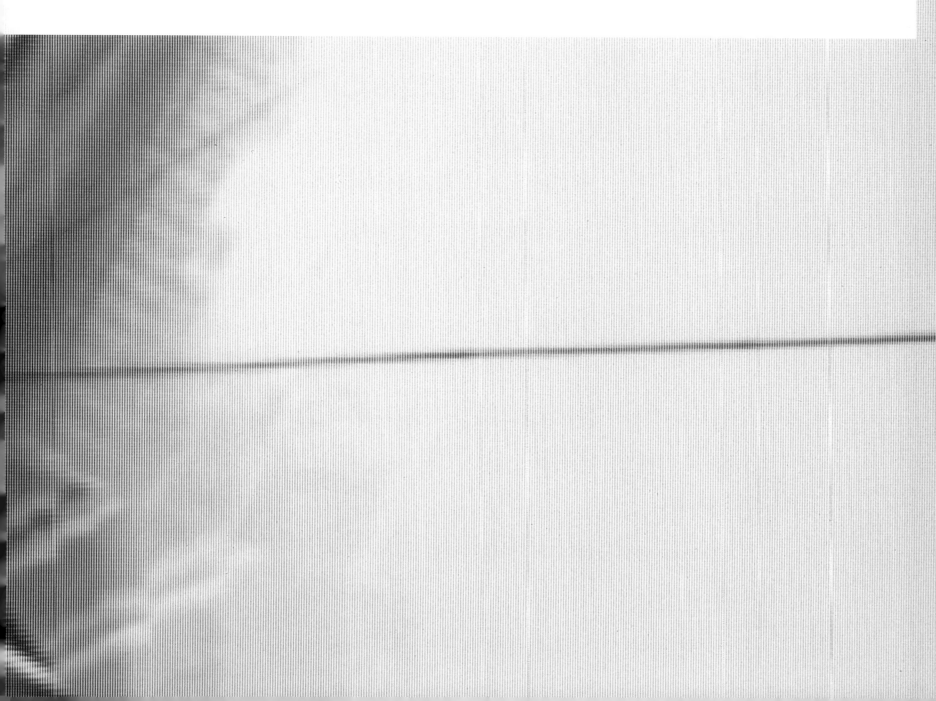

Portable Structures, worldwide, 1987–95

Flexible, touring structures designed by Imagination for presentations and events, which help to circumvent the limitations imposed by existing venues.

Imagination has always been involved in touring exhibitions and environments. For the most part they have been housed within gallery spaces or exhibition halls; occasionally they have utilized more unusual venues – as in the case of a series of travelling exhibitions and entertainments held on trains in the late 70s and early 80s. But these touring exhibitions rely on the existence of other venues – mobile or otherwise – to host them. At Imagination, there is also a long tradition of designing portable structures – freestanding 'buildings' that can move from place to place. Recognizing that even the most conveniently located venue has a limited catchment area, Imagination has regularly explored this aspect of architecture as a hypothetical exercise. Yet possibly the most ambitious portable scheme developed by the company was in response to a specific brief. BT Expo '87, affectionately nicknamed the Slug, was commissioned following the success of Top Telco, a British Telecom staff conference held in 1986. British Telecom asked Imagination to consider ways in which such a large-scale exhibition could be taken on the road, for audiences made up of the general public. Imagination dismissed existing venues as too restrictive and lacking impact, and instead began to work on a portable scheme.

At about the same size as St Paul's Cathedral in plan, the Slug was designed to be the largest touring structure of its type. It was designed as a demountable enclosure that would sit, for twenty-one days out of twenty-eight, at venues such as disused airfields, race tracks or showgrounds on the outskirts of towns; if two structures were simultaneously in use, the turnaround time between closing in one town and opening in the next would be fourteen days – with the structure transported in sections by helicopter. Hosting twelve shows a day, the venue could process up to a million visitors a year. Once there, the audience would find themselves in an immersive experience of the British Telecom brand. The interior would be split into four zones; a main exhibition and reception area, interactive presentation pods, a main auditorium and a secondary exhibition area. Additional facilities would include restaurants and a TV studio. The Slug would travel with a full support team and facility back-up. Toilets, generators, communications centres, administration units, catering and medical facilities all formed part of the infrastructure, as 12 m (39 ft) long mobile units connected to the main enclosure by 'umbilicals'. The Slug was a collaborative effort between architect Ron Herron, Imagination, which commissioned the structure and designed the contents, and the

structural engineers Buro Happold, whose detailed calculations on the project included factors such as wind pressure coefficients, snow-loading and pressure across the inflator fan blades. The main structure would rest on a steel frame levelled on the ground. To that would be attached a truss floor containing water-filled ballast tanks, for stability. The cover of the structure would be a ribbed envelope of high-strength PVC-coated polyester fabric, which could be fully inflated in one hour. Imagination and its partners worked on the project for a year before British Telecom decided that technology and the nature of its business were changing too fast for it to make a substantial investment in the Slug. All was not lost, however. Much of the thinking and calculations that had gone into the project were to resurface in later designs for touring structures, ranging from a Ford presentation space designed to travel the USA to the Sleeping Beauty Castle (see Entertain) which employed the same water-filled ballast tanks to provide stability.

Facing page, sketches of the Slug, designed by Ron Herron and Imagination.

152

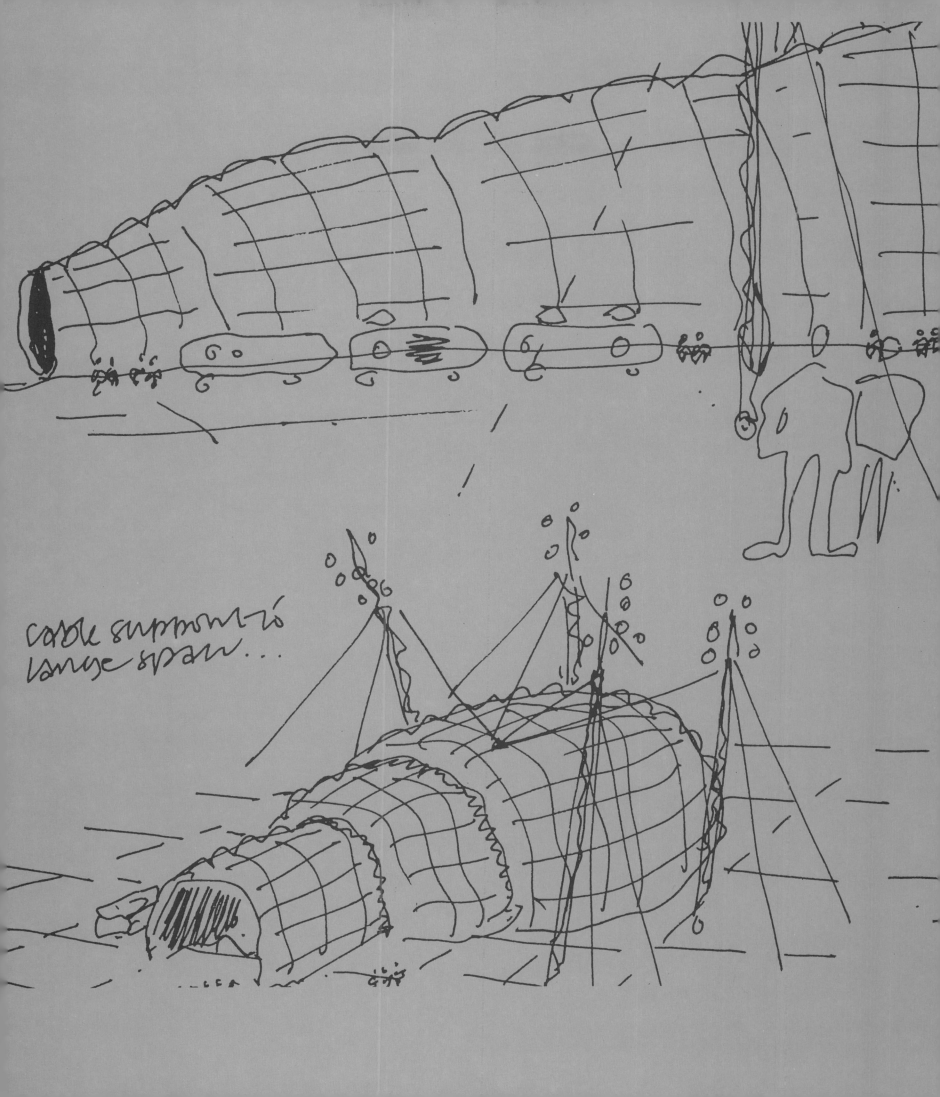

cable supported
large span...

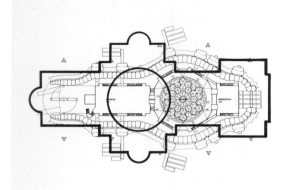

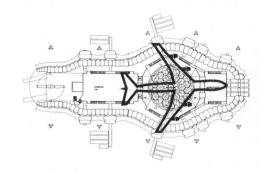

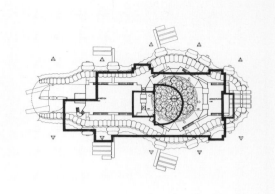

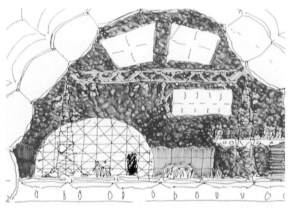

Top, drawings from the presentation document compared the Slug's plan size to that of St Paul's Cathedral, a Boeing 747 and London's Drury Lane Theatre. Above, sketches and renderings of the interior and exterior of the Slug.
Left, model of the Slug.

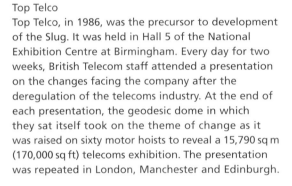

Above and left, the levitating geodesic dome installed in Hall 5 of the NEC for Top Telco. Below, the dome was also used for an Iveco truck launch.

Top Telco

Top Telco, in 1986, was the precursor to development of the Slug. It was held in Hall 5 of the National Exhibition Centre at Birmingham. Every day for two weeks, British Telecom staff attended a presentation on the changes facing the company after the deregulation of the telecoms industry. At the end of each presentation, the geodesic dome in which they sat itself took on the theme of change as it was raised on sixty motor hoists to reveal a 15,790 sq m (170,000 sq ft) telecoms exhibition. The presentation was repeated in London, Manchester and Edinburgh.

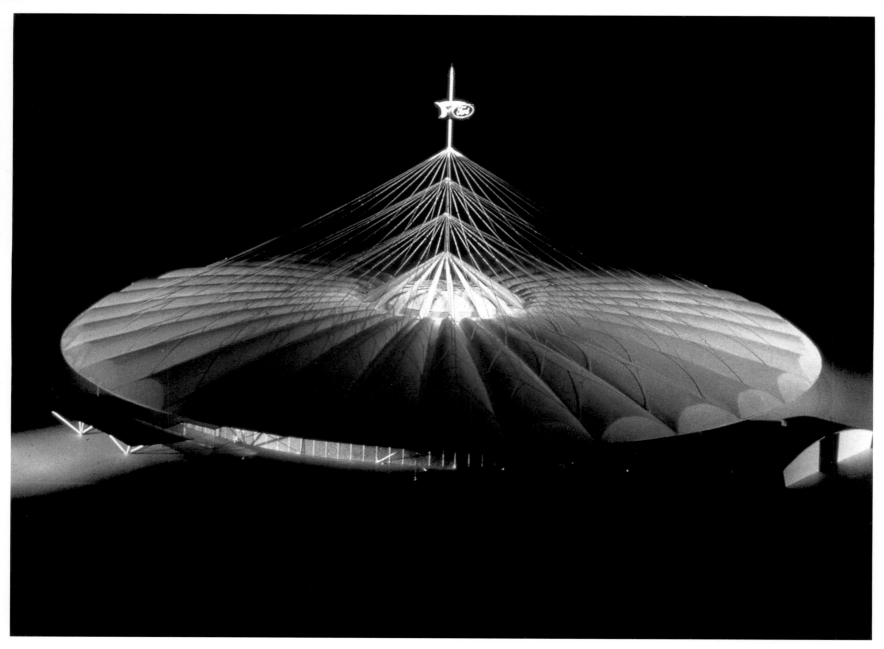

Touring dome
A touring dome structure (1988) was designed to communicate cultural change within Ford to its American dealer body. Having reconnoitred a number of venues across the United States, Imagination felt that they lacked the impact needed by the nature of the presentations, and instead suggested a touring structure designed by Lorenzo Apicella. The concept called for a massive cable net cushion structure, 120 m (394 ft) across, supported by a central mast. The column-free interior was large enough to house three-storey pavilions, and the plans included an auditorium, a theatre, a central piazza and a large exhibition space.

Blue Sky
The 'Blue Sky' research project (1994) was an outline proposal, commissioned by AT&T, to develop an innovative, flexible and touring structure, capable of performing equally well in a city park or a wilderness environment. The building would act as a highly functional research centre while providing a unique expression of the telecoms company's corporate values and philosophy.

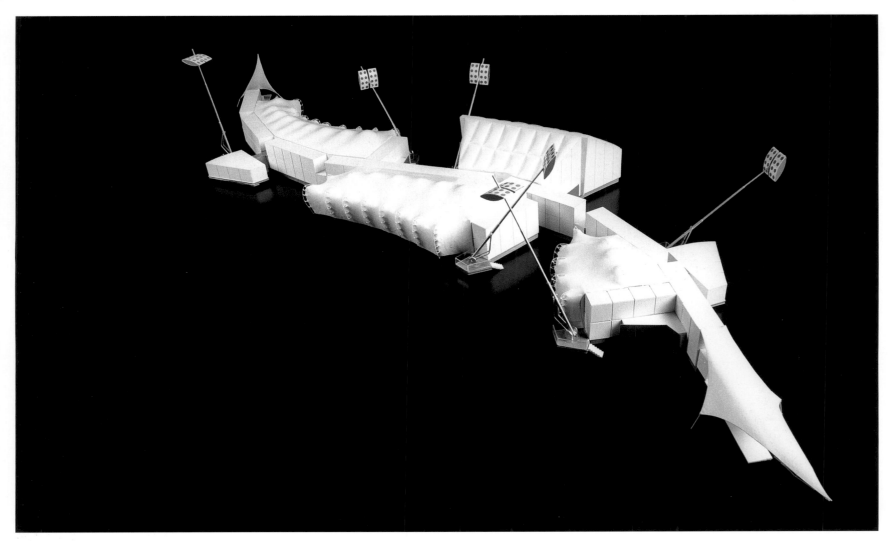

Touring Brand Centre
Originally commissioned by Coca-Cola, the Brand Centre (1995) would utilize a fleet of converted 12 m (40 ft) trailers to provide a flexible and totally self-contained touring brand experience centre, including a dedicated presentation auditorium, exhibition space, broadcast studio and hospitality facilities.

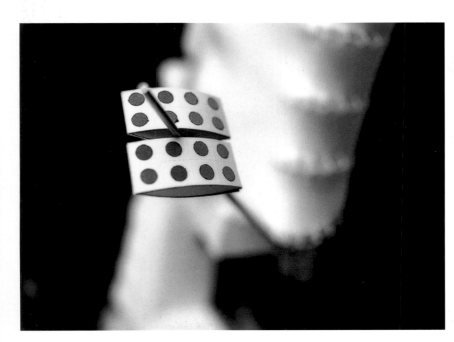

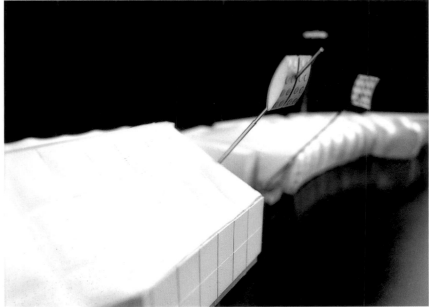

Adventure One
Adventure One (1995) was a self-initiated project undertaken by Imagination as a detailed creative and commercial feasibility study for the development of a flexible and touring brand communication platform through the customization of seventy standard 12 m (40 ft) trailers. At each location, the trailers would be joined together to form a large and flexible environment. All additional equipment required to mount shows and presentations would also be transported within the same trailers.

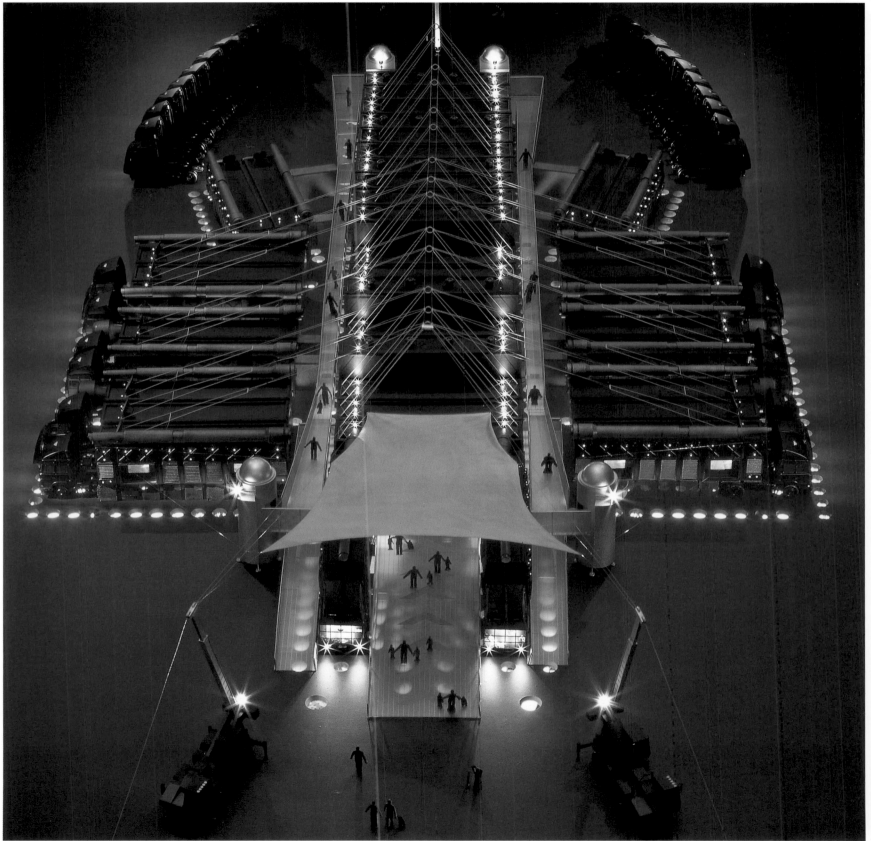

Ford Orion Launch, Northampton, 1982

A sophisticated architectural illusion was created to add
an element of surprise to the launch of the Ford Orion.

Throughout its early years, much of Imagination's best-known work was for spectacular product launches. One of its main clients in this area was Ford, for whom the company had designed and produced car launches since the late 70s, always trying to top the last event – if not in terms of scale or budget, then certainly by giving the audience a day to remember. Early landmarks included the launch of the Ford Sierra in London's Docklands, for which 1,000-seat auditoriums were mounted on tracks and moved up and down a line of warehouses during the launch, and the fourteen-country launch of the Cargo truck for which Imagination virtually reconstructed a conference venue in Montreux, Switzerland. Surprise and spectacle were key elements of each event, but they were also underpinned by relevance to current business issues. When Imagination was asked to launch the new Ford Orion, Ogilvy & Mather's advertising strapline – 'A modern variation on a classical theme' – provided the business angle. With reference to the strapline, Ford had requested that the launch be held at a stately home. Imagination had advised that few, if any, stately homes were designed to handle car launches with an audience of 500, but in the end, a researcher chanced upon Castle Ashby, the sixteenth-century seat of Lord Northampton.

Every night for a week, a group of 500 Ford dealers and their spouses left a business meeting in London, boarded a specially chartered Pullman train, and travelled to Northampton, where they were met by a fleet of coaches and driven to Castle Ashby. There, they were led into the splendid surroundings of the castle – replete with Grinling Gibbons carvings and Old Masters on the walls – and offered a drink before being ushered into the ballroom, where they sat down to dinner, slightly bemused at the lack of any obvious space in which to reveal the new car. At the end of the meal, during brandy and cigars, the managing director stood up and gave a short speech, ending with the words, 'Sit back and enjoy these classical surroundings.' At that moment, the lights in the room went out, and shafts of eerie blue light began to appear through the floor. Suddenly, the entire side wall of the room flew out and upwards, leaving a 37 by 6 m (120 by 20 ft) hole in the side of the building and allowing a blast of cool, evening air into the room. As jaws dropped, the London Symphony Orchestra struck up. Meanwhile, a vast circular projection screen, showing a film of the car being driven through the same gates through which they had come just hours before, appeared to levitate across the gardens towards the castle. In the distance, a fireworks display began as three

cars on scissor jacks began to rise into the room, immediately in front of the astonished audience. As a finishing touch, lights positioned across miles of Capability Brown-designed parkland were switched on to illuminate the countryside. What the dealers had not realized was that the ornate, 500-seat ballroom in which they had spent the evening was in fact an elaborate fake, and that they were not sitting in the sixteenth-century castle at all. Instead, the mock-ballroom was constructed within a large steel box frame, connected directly to the rear of the castle, and extending over the North lawn at first floor level. Although the ballroom was a temporary structure, it had to meet the same fire and safety regulations as a permanent construction. Despite such modern requirements, it was essential that the ballroom should look as authentic as possible in order to maintain the illusion. To that end, original oil paintings and furniture were borrowed from the castle's collection, while chandeliers, mouldings and other details were specially made. The wall itself was lifted by means of a traditional theatrical flytower and a 15-ton counterweight – hydraulic rams and other solutions having been rejected due to expense. The revelation that the ballroom was not so much a room as a stage had the effect of turning the audience themselves into 'actors' on that stage – unwitting participants in an all-encompassing performance which had begun when they boarded the train.

Challenges

Staging such an event on a working estate, and centred around a listed sixteenth-century castle, threw up several unique challenges: the ballroom and its steel frame had to be constructed and dismantled in a comparatively short period – six weeks including a week of shows – without damaging the castle. Furthermore, all catering and services had to be managed without recourse to the castle's own facilities, and power had to be supplied by generators in the surrounding farmers' fields. One of the more unusual inclusions in the final budget was a bill for £660 for loss of milk yield from cows disturbed by the fireworks.

Above, the sequence of events experienced by visitors. Below, far left the 'ballroom' under construction. The local planning authority only granted permission for such an unusual temporary structure on the grounds that Castle Ashby's fee would be used to pay for repairs to its roof. Below, the cars on scissor jacks.

Millennium Central, Birmingham, 1995
Proposals for a ground-breaking visitor attraction
to mark the turn of the Millennium.

The six weeks during the summer of 1995 in which Imagination had to prepare concept presentations for the Millennium exhibition were the busiest the company has ever had. It was also, perhaps, the time that it worked most effectively as a multi-disciplinary team; architects, graphic designers, writers and film directors, as well as logistics teams and production managers worked flat-out to compile the enormous array of information needed to satisfy the Millennium Commission. Imagination's belief was that pre-determined exhibitions, designed for people to 'go and see', belonged to the past. The turn of the Millennium called for a newer, more ambitious approach, in tune with our hopes for the future. The proposal was for a continuously evolving Millennium destination, opening in the year 2000, that would be the finale to a three-year programme of activity in which every person in Britain would be invited to make their contribution to a shared Millennium Experience. The effect was to galvanize the Millennium Commissioners, some of whom had previously doubted the viability of a great exhibition. Here, they could see, was a company with a clear vision of what the Millennium celebrations could be; it was an exciting, inspiring vision – of Millennium Central, a place that was awesome and new, symbolizing a country re-energized and re-orientated by this landmark in time.

Time was to be the theme of Millennium Central. At the National Exhibition Centre in Birmingham, ten glass-and-steel pavilions, each focusing on a different interpretation of Time, would be configured along a mile-long Avenue of Time, with a performance area – Show Time – at one end and a Tower of Time at the other. Attached to the back of each pavilion would be a Millennium Sphere, a mobile exhibition space which in the three years leading up to the exhibition would travel the country, gathering regional contributions on art, science, sport, environment, theatre, entertainment, business, before being reassembled at Millennium Central. Alternative architectural schemes were drawn up for the other three sites under consideration, and when the Millennium Commission announced that the exhibition would be sited on the meridian at the Greenwich Peninsula, a further two pavilions were added and the buildings were reconfigured as the Circle of Time, the world's largest clock face. Imagination had worked with the Richard Rogers Partnership to ensure that the requirements of Millennium Central would fit in with the architects' existing masterplan for the site. Siting the exhibition at Greenwich involved higher costs than Birmingham and the two firms

began to collaborate to find the most cost-effective way to house the exhibition. From these discussions came the concept of a fabric dome structure to house the themed pavilions. Not long afterwards, in early 1997, Imagination decided to stand back from the project, believing that delays in appointing a suitable operator and changes to the business plan made its original creative proposals undeliverable.

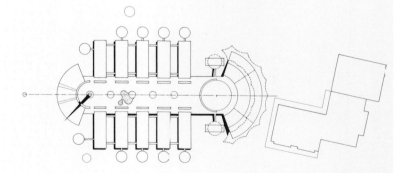

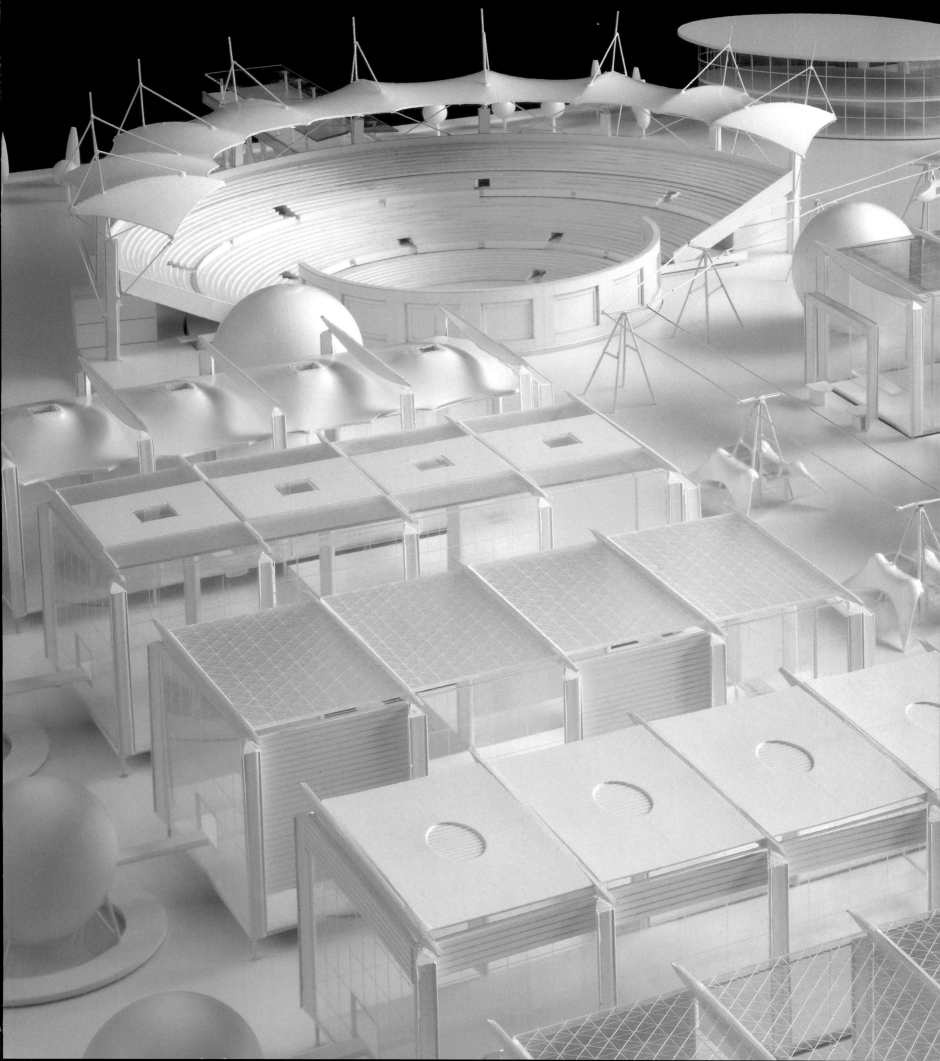

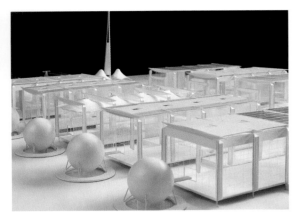
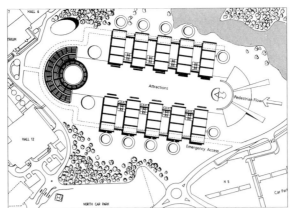
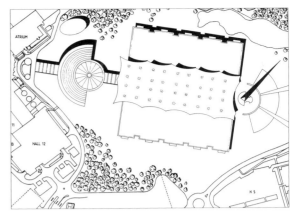

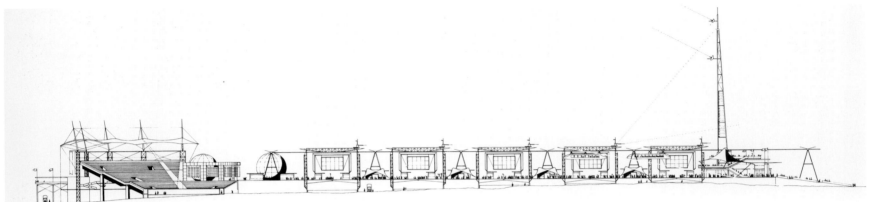

Above and below, model, plans and renderings
from Imagination's concept presentation.

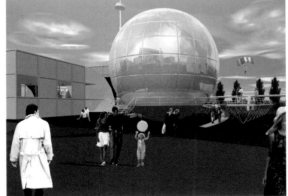

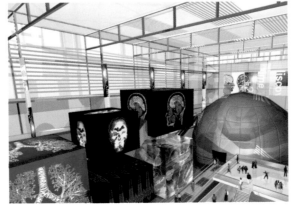

Identity

Imagination developed a complete corporate identity for Millennium Central, including logo, colour palette and application guidelines for an enormous range of media, from stationery, merchandise and phone cards to wayfinding signage and the livery of the monorail system that was to provide on-site transportation. The fact that Imagination had rendered or fabricated many of these examples added to the richness of its concept presentation, allowing the Millennium Commissioners a window onto an attraction so completely described that it appeared to already exist, making it easier for them to agree to the proposals.

Above, applications of the logo and identity on monorail livery, signage and merchandise, including chocolate bars and stationery illustrated with two cartoon badgers, Mill e and Lennie. Left, rendering of the Show Time arena at Millennium Central. Below left, rendering showing a Millennium Sphere on tour. Below right, concept drawing of an attraction at Millennium Central.

BT VE Day Celebrations, London, 1995

A spectacular lighting and fireworks display to commemorate the end of World War II in Europe.

In May 1995, a two-day event in London's Hyde Park marked the fiftieth anniversary of VE day, the end of the Second World War in Europe. The executive producer of the event, Major Michael Parker, had a long-standing association with Imagination, having worked with the company on the Great Children's Party for the Queen's Silver Jubilee in 1977. He approached Imagination, needing a dramatic finale for the two-day event. Imagination, meanwhile, had been in discussions with its client BT about how it might support the event, and put the two together. BT's requirements were simple: first, that whatever was done in its name should win 'front page' newspaper and TV coverage, and second, that it should be in sympathy with the spirit of the moment. Thoughts of sponsoring the entertainment stages or providing facilities in the park were dismissed as lacking impact. Attention turned to the 188 m (620 ft) Telecom Tower. Five years earlier, Imagination had lit the tower for a spectacular event publicizing BT's phone code changes, broadcast on television. The Telecom Tower, however, was several miles from the centre of the action in Hyde Park. It was decided that the two could be linked by a laser, ignited by the Queen, which would be, in turn, the cue for lighting 2,000 telecommunications towers and bonfire beacons across Britain; in a neat parallel, beacons had been lit to mark the end of the war fifty years earlier.

The audience for the display was two-fold: 200,000 people in the park, and a live television audience. Imagination worked with the BBC to choreograph a sequence using several camera positions in which footage of the Queen speaking would be intercut with images of the Telecom Tower glowing with light, thereby creating a dramatic build-up to the firing of the laser and the firework display which followed, which would be visible to the audience in the park. In the hours before the laser struck the top of the Telecom Tower, launching the spectacular finale, the tower had been pulsing with light from top to toe. The display centred on a red, blue and white lighting sequence generated from a combination of four sites at the tower's base and sixteen architectural luminaires on the tower itself. Its central core was lit by 280 Par 64s, whilst the satellite station half-way up the tower was lit from above with twenty red floodlights. Four Sky-Arts provided a searchlight effect in the sky. To create an appropriate backdrop, four riggers had worked twelve hours a day for two weeks to cover the tower with 2,530 sq m (27,220 sq ft) of white industrial vinyl. They also attached over a kilometre (0.62 miles) of Arcline sequential linear strobe tubing laid vertically down the length of the building, which created a chase sequence, mimicking the effect of water pouring down the tower, while twenty-four Cyberlights projected moving images of the BT piper logo onto its sides. The firework display lasted just fifteen seconds, but at a rate of over eighteen shells per second, it included over 280 bursts. In order to counter fears that a stray firework might fall on surrounding buildings, Imagination arranged to make a donation to a firemen's charity, in exchange for the presence of off-duty firemen on the nearby roof-tops.

Croydon Lighting Scheme, Croydon, 1993
Concept for an architectural lighting scheme that would
give Croydon town centre a unique night-time identity.

Joy to the World, London, 1988–1992
For five consecutive years, Imagination worked with Major Michael
Parker to transform the Royal Albert Hall for a celebration of Christmas
performed 'in the round'. Held in aid of Save the Children, the show
was broadcast live by the BBC.

Ford Fiesta Launch, London, 1989

Every day for a week, 800 people entered the London Arena via a specially constructed tunnel, and took their seats facing floor-to-ceiling projection screens. After a brief presentation, the screens tracked out to reveal the arena, into which two car transporters and forty-seven Fiestas drove, before executing a seven-minute choreographed display while overhead a 'ceiling' of projection screens undulated in wave formations.

Around the World in 80 Days, London, 1992

A performance of a new musical, *Around the World in 80 Days*, was held at the Royal Albert Hall to celebrate the 40th anniversary of Holiday Inn. The show featured acts from around the world, including the band of the Coldstream Guards, the Chinese State Circus and Caribbean carnival dancers. As a finale, the stage was transformed into a giant three-tier birthday cake, on which a hundred top-hatted tap dancers performed.

Around the World in 80 Days, London, 1992

An Ideas Company

Perspective: J Mays

'Imagination is an ideas company. If there's a hierarchy, it's creativity before execution. That's one of the reasons I enjoy going there – because I feel stimulated creatively.'

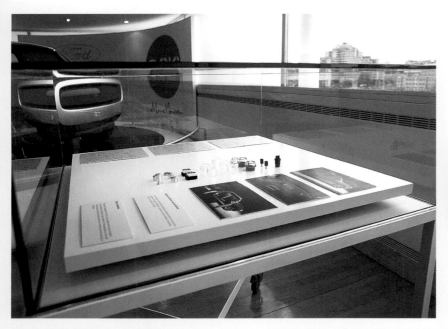

J Mays began his career in Germany as an Exterior Designer with both Audi AG and BMW AG, before returning to the USA as the Chief Designer in Volkswagen of America's Design Center in California, where he was responsible for the design and branding of the Volkswagen Concept 1, the precursor to the new Beetle. In 1993, Mays returned to Audi AG in Germany as Design Director, before changing direction in his career by joining SHR Perceptual Management as Vice President of Design Development. In 1997 he became Vice President, Design, Ford Motor Company, at which time he began to work with Imagination on wide variety of projects.

Above, an installation in London's Design Museum created to temporarily house the 021C concept car designed by Marc Newson.

'I am not a logistics person,' says J Mays. 'I'm an ideas person, a big picture person. When I'm first trying to do something, I'm not interested in how it's going to get done, I'm interested in whether the idea is effective. If you're always worried about how to execute something, you're locking yourself into a very small box.' New ideas and experiment have figured large throughout Mays' career as an automotive designer. He was responsible for the Audi AVUS concept car, and for the Volkswagen Concept 1, the precursor to the new Beetle, and since joining Ford Motor Company as Vice President, Design, in 1997, he has led the development of a number of revolutionary concept vehicles including the 24/7 Internet car and the futuristic 021C, designed by Marc Newson.

Mays' role as the head of design at Ford Motor Company takes him around the world, moving between his own base in Detroit, Michigan and facilities such as the Ghia studio in Italy and studios in the UK, directing the efforts of an international team of 900 designers. One of his regular stops, every couple of months or so, are the London offices of Imagination, with whom he has developed a close collaborative relationship which began shortly after his appointment, when he worked with the company on the design and development of the Trustmark stand at the 1998 North American International Auto Show.

Although he enjoyed actually executing something on that scale – 'it's much larger than an automobile,' he jokes – more interesting 'was the development of the strategy as it started to take shape. The interesting thing Imagination brought to the table was its ability to strategize, not only about what the brand was today, but about whether the brand could ultimately be more.' The following two years produced a diverse array of projects – from exhibition stands to a museum installation, films and multimedia presentations, and even a new automotive concept – but the strategic, free-thinking sessions Mays enjoyed with Imagination on the Detroit stand laid the foundations for a collaborative relationship that is fundamentally about generating ideas. 'Imagination,' says Mays, 'is an ideas company. The over-riding feeling you get coming out of Imagination is one of creativity. If there's a hierarchy, it's creativity before execution.'

The physical properties of Imagination – its size, its building, its equipment and facilities – have arguably come about to cope with the demands of actually delivering work, but in its culture and ethos, Mays perceives a number of elements which combine to create a fertile environment for the generation of ideas. An important part of his own relationship with the company, he says, is the rapport generated between client and design company, which allows for a frank exchange of views: conversations with Imagination's creative director, Adrian Caddy, usually 'end with us telling each other we're full of it,' but the balance of views and the freedom felt by both design company and client to express them 'usually produces the right result.' Beyond the personal enjoyment Mays gets from such a friendly relationship, he suggests that the informality the company has maintained as both Imagination, its clients and their budgets have got bigger is creatively critical, as it gives the company license to think unbidden on behalf of its clients. Aware of this potential, Mays has encouraged it: 'The way I like working with them is to give them a lot of free reign,' he says, 'because there are a lot of ideas that come out of the company and I don't want to be the big corporation that dictates what it wants from the start. We don't have such an ego here that we'd say unless an idea is originated here, it's not a good idea.' Whether sanctioned or not, Imagination has never been backwards about coming forwards. When it set up its Brand Development Group in 1993, its task was to think proactively for its clients about how they might communicate, and then try to sell the ideas to them. For Mays, Imagination's culture of thinking for itself, facilitated by the informal nature of the relationship they have developed, is extremely valuable.

By way of example, he describes a typical meeting: 'I have dinner with Adrian every couple of months when I'm in London, and part of that is talking about what we've been up to personally, and part of it is talking about what projects we're working on and what projects we're going to start. Those meetings are what I would call creative spark meetings: there's a great creative back and forth that happens, and very often by the end of the meal we've come up with far more projects than we could ever do.' The fact that 'most of them are completely unachievable' does not seem to worry Mays. 'So we think, alright, we haven't got the money to do that, how do we get 90 per cent of the idea across?'

This shared tendency to shoot for the moon, and make mental space for apparently wild ideas is another quality Mays feels helps to foster an atmosphere in which more workable ideas take shape. 'Of course Gary has a business to run,' he says, 'and he has to make a profit, but that's not the impression you get when you walk in the door. It's all about creativity.' Imagination's belief in the value of experiment, evidenced not least by its long tradition of prototyping portable structures and the existence of an in-house technical research and development department, has added a new dimension to Mays' relationship with the company as he involves it in the left-field projects he runs as an enjoyable aside to his main responsibilities. 'I always like to have several projects in the year that are experiments,' he explains. 'They don't need to be expensive projects, but they need to be pushing the boundaries of what is considered the norm. And we always have a couple of projects like that going with Imagination.' Norico.com is one such example. As a promotional tool for the 021C concept car, Imagination developed a pop video, featuring Manga-style animated versions of Robert Palmer and Japanese singer Norico singing The Beatles' 'Drive My Car'. 'The idea of a music video for the 021C is an interesting idea as an experiment,' says Mays. 'It's not extremely costly but it's fun, and it opens our eyes to a new way of communicating.'

Before the idea for the 021C music video emerged, Imagination had co-ordinated the launch of the car on the stand it designed for the Tokyo Motor Show, created a CD-ROM and designed an installation for its temporary residence in London's Design Museum. While the hierarchy may put creativity before execution, Imagination's ability to execute projects in so many different media plays its own part in unlocking new ideas. The very broadness of the multi-disciplinary resource – what Mays describes as a 'medialab' – which enables the company to physically execute so much varied work, itself opens up new creative possibilities, allowing Mays to consider things he wouldn't otherwise: he cites as a further example a film Imagination made to promote the new Thunderbird within Ford.

'As a designer I've got a pretty good idea, when creating a product, of how I'd like that product communicated. But I probably wouldn't have dreamed of doing a film for Thunderbird if Imagination hadn't had the in-house resource to do it,' he says. Not only could Imagination technically produce a film, but because it is connected to the brand through having produced communication for it in so many other media, 'there's a continuity that runs from concept to environment to advertising,' says Mays. 'In the case of Thunderbird, getting the music and the images and the environment around that car right was very important, and I think we were really on one wavelength as we got into that film. And because of that, the message of that film was in direct parallel to the message that the car gives off, which is about optimism, and a nice little piece of American history.'

The combined qualities of Imagination, its informality, openness to experiment and the ability to work across disciplines add up for Mays to a package that enables creative adventure. 'I love it when we start off projects and we don't know where we're going,' he enthuses. 'Working at a gut level, knowing that something good is going to come out of it but not exactly sure what. That's a great way to work.'

Below, top row, stills from Norico.com, the animated pop video produced to promote the 021C concept car. Below, bottom row, screen grabs from a CD-ROM designed to promote the 021C.

Evolve

Imagination evolves to tackle new opportunities; the constant search for new ideas and addition of creative people skilled in an ever-wider variety of disciplines is the means to an end – the ability to meet fresh challenges.

Imagination, 1978 – 2000

Perspective: Gary Withers

'Any successful multi-disciplinary group relies on individual skill, talent, flair, opinion and personality, that's harnessed collectively to produce the best result.'

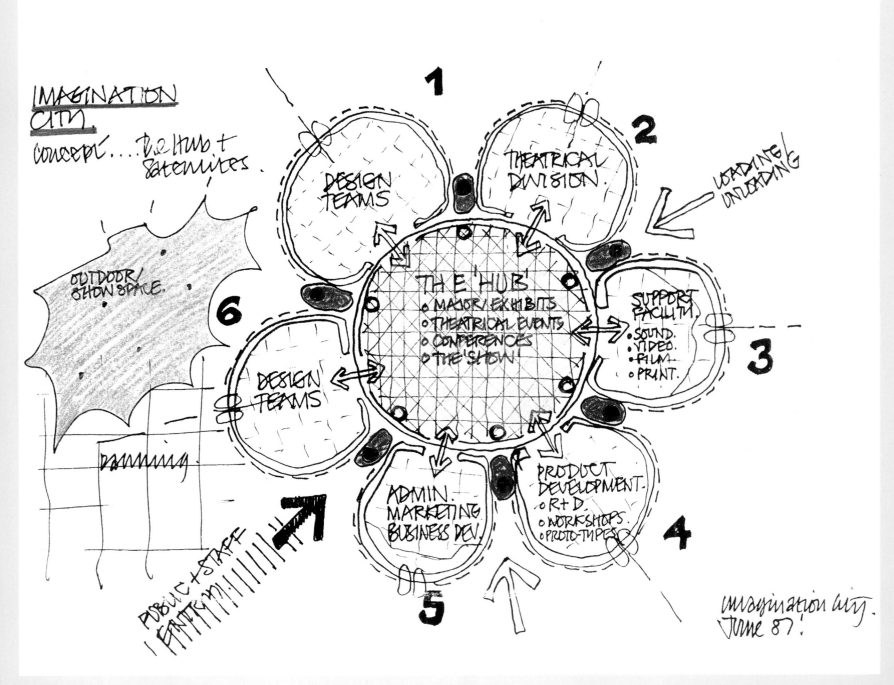

Sketch by Ron Herron showing one of a number of schemes for Imagination City, a multi-disciplinary creative community.

The story of Imagination's growth, and something of its ethos, is told by its offices. In 1978, the young team moved into premises in Marylebone Road. As the company continued to grow, Gary Withers made plans to expand the offices but was pre-empted by a fire that gutted the building. An empty building in Carlisle Street, Soho, sufficed for a few months, before they settled in a bigger building in Maiden Lane, Covent Garden. Rapidly outgrowing its building, the company expanded into the building next door, and then even into a tented structure in the back yard, but even this arrangement was too confined to keep the company, by now thirty-strong, in Maiden Lane for long. Within three years, Imagination had moved again, to Bedford Street in Covent Garden, a grand four-storey building now occupied by another company in the Imagination Group. The move to Bedford Street in 1983 represented a considerable investment for the young company. 'It was scary,' remembers Withers, but the move allowed for continued growth and within six years the company had outgrown Bedford Street. This time, however, Withers was expecting it and had been at work with Ron Herron since 1985 on schemes for a possible replacement. In 1989, Imagination moved into the fifth of those schemes, its current offices on Store Street.

Imagination has always had a strong sense of the *genius loci*, and the opening of the Imagination Building in 1989 confirmed this. It also drew Imagination into the public spotlight, not just as a place but as a phenomenon. Already well known in the design world, Imagination was now taking its vision to a wider public. The awards for the building reflected its innovative architecture, but what was equally innovative was the kind of design and communications company Imagination was – and still is. Unlike companies with either a highly visible leader, or a strong base in formal graphic design or architecture, or hyper-organized management and research procedures, Imagination just seemed to do things, and do them with vigour, at speed, and around a sense of excitement. The building had been transformed in no time at all, and yet it wasn't a traditional studio or office. It was a place where things happened. It was also the first physical expression of a culture that Withers had developed in Imagination, and one that had been in the planning for many years: 'The original idea for a design community started many years ago when I decided that the best thing we could do was buy a mews in Kensington,' Withers explains. 'The idea was that we'd buy both sides of the mews and enclose it. Each mews house would be a different department – a design studio, an audio-visual department, a film department, a model-making department and so on – and you'd have a street which was the common place.'

Arranged across two six-storey buildings on either side of an enclosed street, the Imagination Building today works in almost the same way. The idea behind it now, as then, is 'the brood hen instinct. I wanted to take all these different talents and provide an environment where they could all bustle and rub shoulders and benefit,' says Withers. Co-operative working across creative disciplines is the bedrock on which Imagination is built. In response to every brief, the company assembles a multi-disciplinary team from which emerges a core idea. The team is then re-engineered to deliver a multi-faceted response to the brief. 'I think any successful multi-disciplinary group, like Cirque du Soleil, like the Bauhaus, like us, relies on individual skill, talent, flair, opinion and personality, that's harnessed collectively to produce the best result,' Withers explains. 'That's the trick. I believe that anyone running a multi-disciplinary company must understand that the lighting designer can have the idea, the clown can have the idea, the costume designer can have the idea, the director can have the idea. It doesn't matter who has the idea.' In delivering Imagination's projects, says Withers, everybody's contribution is equal by default. 'You can have a fantastic idea for the Olympics, where the torch comes out of the water and slides up the side of the hill,' he suggests, 'but if it gets stuck, it doesn't matter how good the idea was. Why did it stick? You're only as good as the people who build it, or install it, or wire it. Which is why they're always the most important people. You couldn't build a pyramid without the man who put the fourth block on the second level.'

Withers has a strong belief in the ability of the people around him, and believes that his own role is to encourage them to exceed their own expectations: 'It's very much about having people believe that they are in themselves capable of doing something, and creating an environment in which that can blossom,' he says. 'Because the moment you let them think that perhaps they can't, then they never do anything. I think that the confidence that you can radiate to people helps them. If this was *Star Wars* I'd be holding the light sabre saying "the Force is with you," because they *can* do it; if you believe in people, they'll believe in themselves. It's perfectly possible for anybody to do what they want to do within a culture that allows them to do it.'

The ability to do anything is core to Imagination's identity, informing even the company's name: when, in 1978, Withers staged a management buy out of a design firm he had started, Saffron Design Associates, the company needed a new name. The choice of 'Imagination', the product of a brainstorming session at the Intercontinental Hotel on Hyde Park Corner, lubricated by Tequila Sunrises, says a lot about Withers' intentions for the future. 'I didn't want to us be "architects and interior designers," I didn't want us to be "graphic designers," I didn't want to be "visual something or others,"' he remembers. 'I said, "What we need is a name with a bit of imagination … Ahh, that's it."'

The evocative ambiguity of the name may have signalled Withers' intent to work in whichever disciplines he chose as Imagination, but in Saffron Design Associates, he already had the blueprint for the company Imagination would be over twenty years later. The sum total of its output over the course of its existence to date constitutes a huge body of work of extraordinary diversity, and yet the threads that run through its portfolio can be traced back to its earliest days. As Saffron Design Associates, the company worked across creative disciplines, producing film and graphics alongside three-dimensional environments and theatrical performances. Over the following two decades it merely added to its capabilities to the point where there is little Imagination and its associate companies in the Imagination Group have not tackled, from advertising to corporate identity, architecture to furniture design.

Only recently, having defied categorization for many years, has Imagination put a name to what it does, and it is appropriately loose and unconfining: it is a creator of 'experiences' that can happen anywhere from the aisle of a supermarket to the Royal Albert Hall, a moving train to a disused factory, a six-storey brand centre to an underground car park, magically transformed for one week only into an amazing theme park ride. For all the apparent disparateness of the company's portfolio, the key to it, according to Withers, is the desire to make connections between people. 'Face-to-face dialogue and meeting places are very important. If you went back through architecture you'd have the mound that they all met on in druid times, you'd have the squares where they all promenaded in Edwardian times, you'd have the districts like Soho or Greenwich Village that people meet and congregate in. Connections are what makes the world go round.'

Of all the stages of developing and delivering an Imagination project, from idea through design to construction, Withers' own favourite is 'seeing the satisfaction of people, whether they be a client or a member of the audience. There was a really touching moment after fourteen weeks of misery, pain, worry and fear, doing the Sleeping Beauty Castle, on the first morning in Leipzig when the kids were just coming out of the mist swirling around the town square. It was an amazing feeling to stand there and think "We've brought this together and people are really moved by it." With the lifting wall at Castle Ashby it was very interesting to watch a really hard nosed audience, who had seen endless big launches from us, and knew something was going to happen. They were genuinely gobsmacked. There's a great sense of satisfaction when you know that you've done it and that people are enjoying it. One of the things that has given me a lot of pleasure over the years is that we constantly seek to surprise people. We surprised people with Lloyd's lighting. We surprised people the first year we put the tree in the atrium – how the hell did they get a 100 ft tree inside the building? That's important to me; I think "We'll show 'em."' Withers has a keen sense of what it takes to surprise and impress and is uncompromising in his desire to see it done right. 'Look at the lighting of the Hoover building,' he says. 'It's bright green. I can remember the conversation we had about that: They were all saying "Oh no, it's got to be blue," and I said "It's art deco. What colour is art deco? It's green." "Can't do it green." Why not? It is green, and it stands out.'

Making connections on a grand scale is what Withers intends to do in the next phase of Imagination's growth, Imagination City. The ambitious concept – for an entire living, working creative community 'about the size of a small town' –

has again been in the planning stages for years: it informed some of Herron's schemes in the 1980s, and in a sense Imagination's current headquarters might be seen as a prototype version. Like the building, Imagination City would physically express the company's beliefs. Teamwork, however, would not be between individual designers from different disciplines but between the R&D departments of whole companies. 'All of these big brands are desperate to have a better dialogue with the consumer,' explains Withers, 'but they all do it in isolation. Ford car designers are talking to the youth market, Coca-Cola is talking to the youth market. If you put the drink manufacturer together with the car manufacturer you might end up with a better car.' Alongside the work there would be elements of play – the city would be a public/private place along the lines of Disney's EPCOT centre – and education. As Withers says, 'it would be a place where people can come and learn, and it doesn't matter if they've got a qualification or not; if they've got the enthusiasm then you bring them to the party. It would be a very good way of practically helping to constantly deliver good people.' Again, says Withers, this is merely an escalation of the way Imagination already operates: 'We've done it unofficially for years: if you go back through Imagination's history, and look at the number of people who've come, learnt, left, and often come back, it's a phenomenal impact that we've made on people.'

It seems like a utopian ideal, but is it feasible? If one thinks of Imagination City as a metaphor for how Withers believes large multi-disciplinary company such as Imagination should function, such considerations are irrelevant. But it is not a metaphor. 'It isn't anything that couldn't be done in one step from where we are now,' he says. 'The easiest place to build it would be a lump of flat green land somewhere, but the idea of a regenerated city site, of which there are many, is quite interesting. The problem, as always, is how do you finance it? But I think there's an increasing willingness for large multinational corporations, the fabric of the world's nations, to think about funding something like that. They all know that things have got to change.' The people with whom Withers suggests he might create Imagination City are those with whom Imagination has made connections over twenty-five years: its clients, of course, but also the huge range of architects, property developers, engineers and other specialists with whom it has collaborated on projects that were equally ambitious in their own way. Withers makes Imagination City sound possible, which of course, he believes it is. After all, he says, 'You can do anything, given the right climate, so when people say "it can't be done," I always say "Nothing's impossible."'

Evolution

A representative selection of projects showing Imagination's work and development over the period 1976 to 2000.

1976–79

1
Conference for toy manufacturer Rovex.

2, 3
Bird's Eye Wall's conference at the Bloomsbury Theatre, London.

4, 5
Courtaulds conference at Kensington Town Hall, London.

6, 7
The launch of motor manufacturer British Leyland, held in an aircraft hangar.

8, 9
Visuals from toy company Dunbee Combex Marx's Silver Jubilee exhibition, held in a temporary structure erected in Hyde Park.

10, 11
Scalextric visitor attraction for children, staged on board a British Rail train which toured the UK.

12, 13
Installation and projections for Courtaulds' showrooms in Hanover Square, London, to promote its new fibre, Viloft, to staff, customers and the media.

14
One of a succession of displays designed for the John Player's showroom on Oxford Street.

15
CBS Records conference at the Royal Garden, London.

16, 17
K Shoes conference at the Café Royal, London.

18, 19, 20
Set and show for Granada TV Rental conference.

1980–82

1, 2, 3, 4
Event at the Royal Albert Hall for Essex Petroleum. The company dealt in petrol on the market but never owned any physical assets; it achieved the appearance of physical substance through such devices as its sponsorship of the Lotus racing team, arranged by Imagination, and this spectacular event.

5
Conference for shoe retailer Dolcis.

6, 7
Conference for DER designed to reposition the TV rental market.

8, 11
Cyclists demonstrate the product at a Raleigh conference, held at its factory in Nottingham.

9, 10
Bird's Eye conference at the New London Theatre.

12
'Brand Wars', a Lever Bros event held at the Metropole Hotel in Birmingham. The entrance was dressed to look like the approach to 'Churchill's bunker' through a forest.

13, 14
Stage set and graphics for the launch of the Thrust land-speed record-breaking car.

15
London Fashion Week stage set, commissioned by Philbeach Events.

16, 17
Specially designed nose cone and the interior of the KP Adventure Express, a British Rail train adapted to carry a touring visitor attraction in which children could undertake adventures, each related to a brand owned by the snack company KP.

18
Presentation to promote Courtaulds' new fabric Moygashel, held at its Hanover Square showroom.

19
Exhibition stand and audio visual presentation for the Greater London Council stand at the Ideal Home Show.

20, 21
Environment and show for DER conference at the New London Theatre.

1983–85

1, 2
Developers Sunley were finding it hard to let a building on Battersea Bridge, London. Reasoning that its principal quality was that it was cheap, Imagination took potential tenants to a cocktail reception at the Grosvenor House Hotel, before flying them down the Thames in helicopters. On rooftops across London were illuminated signs giving the higher rental prices of buildings and arrows pointing to Battersea. Arriving at the building, they witnessed a spectacular lighting and firework display. The building was let the following day.

3, 4
Guinness conference and show involving 150 performers, held in London's Docklands.

5
Environment for Ford business meeting.

6
Ford Transit launch in Strasbourg. Vast moving projection screens and tracking projection units created an animated backdrop to the presentations.

7
Model showing planned offices for advertising agency Young & Rubicam at the top of London's Black Cat Factory.

8, 9, 10
Rooftop restaurant and exhibition space, and subterranean Disney-style dark ride created in London's Barbican Centre for the launch of the Ford Escort.

11
Exhibit from Ford's stand at the 1985 Barcelona Motor Show.

12, 13, 14
Reveal of Ford's stand at the Birmingham Motor Show.

15
Techline, a touring Ford exhibition on new technologies and work practices, which visited twenty-three Ford plants across Europe.

16
The Greater London Council Thames Barrier Exhibition Centre.

17, 18
Launch of the Ford Granada at Boreham.

19, 20, 21, 22
Costumes and stage set for a musical performed on the National Theatre's Olivier stage for one night only. Staged for a meeting of the Young Presidents' Organisation, the musical was based around the story of London's past, as told by its Lord Mayors.

23, 24
Model showing concept for a touring Marks and Spencer retail outlet.

25
'Ford Gives You More', a touring musical production featuring 100 performers, seen here at Castle Ashby in Northampton.

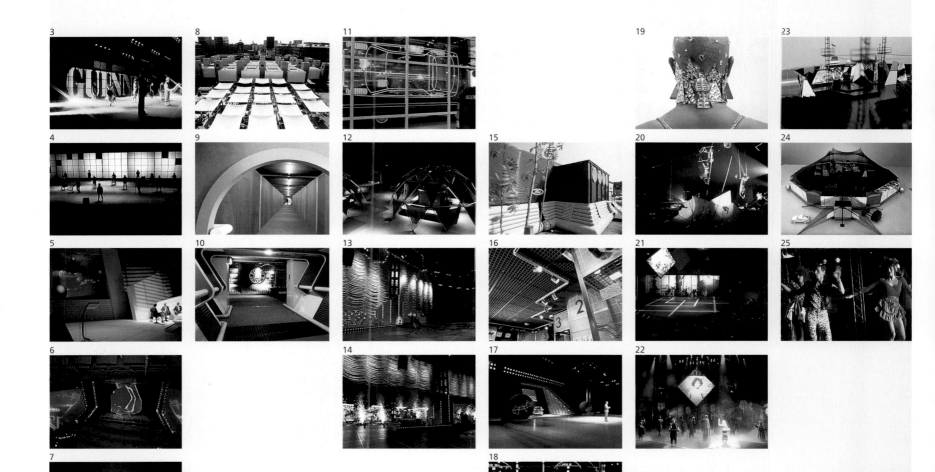

 1

 2

1986

1, 2
Structures designed to host an event marking the merger of Ford and Iveco to form Iveco Ford. The new company's entire range of vehicles, from trucks to fire engines, performed a high-speed, drive-through in the larger structure, while the smaller was used for dinner and entertainments.

3, 4, 5
Sketches and models of a concept for Dutch theme park, Twente Technovia.

6
Concept model for atrium development at the Trocadero Centre in London.

7
Set design for a Gillette razor commercial.

8
A concept for the first British Gas AGM at Birmingham. Delegates would travel by miniature train between the walls which would carry projections.

9
Essex Petroleum event at the Royal Albert Hall. The venue was decorated in the company's corporate colours red, blue and silver, and the terraces were made out of oil drums.

10
Ford Transit launch in Strasbourg.

11
Sketch by Ron Herron of a touring exhibition venue for British Telecom, nicknamed 'the Slug'.

12
Concept model of Waterice, a proposed theme park based around water, snow and ice.

13
Concept model of a visitor centre for the Channel Tunnel.

14
Proposals for a launch event for the Channel Tunnel, to be held in the tunnel itself.

15
Fabric-covered mobile unit for Ford's motor sport team.

16
Concept model of a stage set for the musical *Oliver!* to be performed at the then derelict Lyceum Theatre.

17
Ford stand at the Birmingham Motor Show.

18
Environment designed for the relaunch of the Ford Cargo truck.

19, 20
Ford Retail Development Centre, in the grounds of Castle Ashby.

21
Concept for an exhibition on archaeology at the British Museum, commissioned by the government of Saudi Arabia.

22, 23
Architectural branding exercise for the South Bank Centre in London.

 35

 8

 15

 4

 9

 11

 16

 19

 22

 5

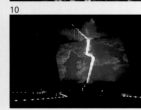 10

 12

 17

 20

23

 6

 13

18

21

 7

 14

1987–88

1
Concept model of an 'adventure' environment designed to host a staff training programme for British Telecom.

2
Concept model of a mobile customer contact centre for Ford.

3
Ford stand at the Belfast Motor Show.

4
Environment for Ford's quarterly business meeting.

5
Ford stand at the Birmingham Motor Show.

6
British Airways' Club Class launch event. Cabin crew from around the world were connected in a live link-up to make the presentation.

7
'Black box' environment within the Cumberland Hotel, London, to house a Trusthouse Forte launch event.

8, 9
Live event for 7,500 British Airways staff staged in an aircraft hangar, designed to reassure and motivate them after the corporate merger with British Caledonian.

10
Concept model for an auditorium at Windsor Safari Park.

11
Wall's Ice Cream sales conference.

12
Proposed redevelopment of the *Mirror* newspaper's former printworks in London as 'Mirror Live', a visitor attraction based on extensions of the Mirror brand.

13, 14, 15
Ford stand at the Brussels Motor Show.

16
Entrance canopy designs for the Telecom Tower in London.

17
Moving graphics used at the end of British Telecom's TV advertisements.

18
'Ford Gives You More' touring musical show at the National Exhibition Centre in Birmingham.

19
Touring product launch for Zanussi. The demountable environment could be assembled in hotel rooms.

Herron Associates at Imagination
From the mid-1980s, architect Ron Herron collaborated with Imagination on a wide variety of projects, including the company's own Store Street offices, completed in 1989. In the same year, Herron merged his practice with Imagination, becoming Herron Associates at Imagination in a partnership that lasted until his death in 1993. As well as built projects, such as the Bone Walk in the Dinosaurs exhibition at London's Natural History Museum, Herron's output at Imagination included a large amount of concept work which helped to reposition the company as a creator of fixed, as well as temporary, facilities.

1989

1, 2, 3, 4
Imagination's Store Street building dressed for the company's surprise tenth anniversary party, held on the roof of the then derelict building. Entertainment was provided by costumed actors mingling with the crowd, sound and light-scapes in the empty interior.

5, 6
The Hazard Dome, commissioned by the Department of Trade and Industry, was a touring exhibition for children providing information on safety risks in the home.

7
Model of Ford's stand at the Birmingham Motor Show.

8
Interior design of the reception area at British Steel's London headquarters.

9, 10
Displays in one of British Telecom's business centres.

11
BT television broadcast. Imagination's Business Television department creates bespoke programming for screening on corporate TV networks.

12
Lighting design scheme for the entrance to London's Waterloo Station.

13
Environmental design for British Steel's Annual General Meeting.

14
Proposal to create a nightclub for cigarette brand Marlboro from a disused factory in Germany.

15, 16
Concept models showing proposed rides at Dutch theme park, De Efteling.

17
Privatization roadshow for the UK's water companies.

18
Concept model of a visitor centre for information technology company ICL.

19
Engine plinth for use on Ford motor show stands.

20
The launch of *Metropolitan Home* magazine, held at the Imagination Gallery.

21, 22, 23
Iveco Ford truck launch at its factory in Langley.

24
Concept model showing the lighting scheme for the exterior of British Steel's headquarters.

25, 26
Launch of the Ford Fiesta at the London Arena in which forty-seven cars performed a seven-minute 'ballet'.

27
Joy to the World, an annual extravaganza broadcast live from the Royal Albert Hall at Christmas, in aid of Save the Children.

28, 29, 30
Stills from *Natural Networking*, a film made for senior executives at AT&T to alert them to the increasing importance of technologies such as the Internet in communications.

31
Concept model showing a lighting scheme for a palace in Abu Dhabi.

Imagination GIC
Based in Imagination's former premises in Bedford
Street, Covent Garden, and Hong Kong, Imagination
Global Investor Communications' eighty staff organize
international financial communications roadshows.
The company pioneered the area in which it
operates, and since 1986 has co-ordinated hundreds
of international roadshows.

1

1990

1
Investor relations roadshow
for the privatization of
the UK's regional electricity
companies.

2, 3
Display concept designed for
installation in airports and
other public spaces to promote
Vogue.

4
The launch of the new look
Ford Escort and Orion in an
environment created at the
National Exhibition Centre,
Birmingham.

5
Environment for Ford's Service
Managers Meeting.

6
Temporary structure designed
for use as a theatre in Covent
Garden during a Summer
festival season.

7
'My Favourite Tree', a *Financial
Times* exhibition held in the
Imagination Gallery.

8, 9
Concept for 'Motown',
a television show based on
Ford products.

10
Ford stand at the Ulster
Motor Show.

11
Ford stand at the Paris
Motor Show.

12, 13, 14
Film created for the launch
of the Ford Escort.

15
La Rouche, a food outlet in the
Arnhem branch of department
store De Bijenkorf, designed
by Virgile & Stone.

16, 17
A televised lighting and
firework display centred on the
Telecom Tower alerted the
public to the London phone
code changes.

18
Portable structure, pictured in
Central Park, New York,
designed to facilitate AT&T's
technological research.

19
The launch of the Tokyo
edition of the *Financial Times*,
held in the Imagination atrium.

20
Architectural lighting scheme
for British Steel's London
headquarters.

21, 22
Joy to the World, an annual
extravaganza broadcast live
from the Royal Albert
Hall at Christmas, in aid of
Save the Children.

23
Interior design for the
reception area at British
Steel's London headquarters.

24, 25
Ford stand at the Turin
Motor Show.

1991

1, 2, 3, 4
Stage set and environment for Ford Business Meeting.

5
Concept for a stage set for use in Disney's touring show, 'Magical Music'.

6, 7
Innovations exhibition at BT's facilities at Martelsham.

8
Ford stand at the London Motor Show.

9
Spread from Ford's *Car Drivers' Guide*.

10
Concept model for a Batman ride at Universal Studios.

11
Still from *Man and Boy*, an in-flight information film for British Airways' First Class passengers.

12
Privatization roadshow for the electricity generating company Powergen.

13, 14
Lighting design proposals for Belfast docks.

15
BT exhibition stand at Geneva Telecom.

16
Exhibit from the Theatre Museum in Covent Garden.

17
Ford stand at the Amsterdam Motor Show.

18
Concept model showing exterior lighting scheme for the Lyceum Theatre, intended for a performance of the musical *Oliver!*.

19
Concept model of a touring structure commissioned by Rank Xerox, designed to showcase its new products.

20
Concept model for a retail development commissioned by Whittle Communications.

21
Products designed as part of a corporate identity created for the Leeds Building Society by Virgile & Stone.

22
Environment for the Midland Electricity Board's Annual General Meeting.

23
Model of the Helena Rubenstein cosmetics counter, designed by Virgile & Stone.

24
Stage set for the Genco share price reveal.

25
Environment for South West Water's Annual General Meeting.

26, 27, 28
Environment for Iveco Ford's Cargo truck launch.

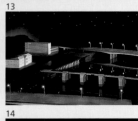

1992

1, 2, 3, 4
'Me and My Body' exhibition at the Eureka! Museum for Children, Halifax, UK. Interactive attractions included the Giant Ear, the Tooth-and-Tongue Machine and The First Step.

5
Model showing proposal to redesign 'Mission to Mars' at Disney World, Florida.

6
Touring exhibition for MTV.

7
Stage set for the privatization roadshow of drug company Wellcome.

8
Proposal to brighten up concourses on British Rail stations.

9
An Arts Council Awards event, held in the Imagination Gallery.

10
Concept model showing proposed headquarters building for Volvo.

11
Event for Holiday Inn, staged in London's Natural History Museum.

12, 13
Ford stand at Birmingham Motor Show. The 10 m sphere housed the Ghia-designed Focus concept car. The exterior of the sphere was used as a projection surface for a constantly changing 'Design and Technology' show.

14
Proposal for a visitor centre at the Sellafield nuclear power plant.

15, 16
Concept model for the stage set of the musical *Heathcliff*.

17
Concept model for a Polaroid exhibition stand at the trade show Photokina.

18
Joy to the World, an annual Christmas extravaganza at the Royal Albert Hall, in aid of Save the Children.

19
Lighting scheme for the Art Deco Hoover Building, now a Tesco supermarket.

20
High street retail concept for Ford.

21
Concept model showing a proposal for a chain of out-of-town Disney retail centres.

22
Model of a proposed Ford launch environment.

23
Concept model of a Ford motor show stand.

24
Ford stand at the Paris Motor Show.

25
Ford stand at the Geneva Motor Show.

26
Concept model for the stage set of the musical *Tutankhamun*.

27
'Dinosaurs', a permanent exhibition at the Natural History Museum in London.

28
The Amsterdam branch of department store De Bijenkorf, designed by Virgile & Stone.

29
Early concept model showing a precursor of the Disney train that runs between Disney World and Miami.

30
Still from *Pure Pleasure*, a film made to accompany the launch of the Ford Probe.

31
The European Commission Pavilion at Expo '92 in Seville. Imagination designed an exhibition on the theme 'Renaissance Europe to European Renaissance', covering 500 years of European history.

32
Model showing detail of a proposed Russian pavilion for Disney's World Showcase at the EPCOT Centre.

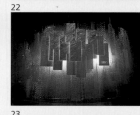

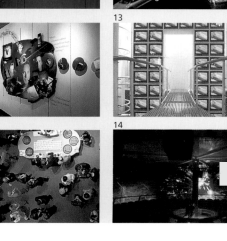

1993

1, 2
Ford stand at the London Motor Show.

3
Stage set and performance for the televized BAFTA Awards ceremony.

4
'Safety Zone', a presentation environment designed for Ford that toured the UK's motorway service stations.

5, 6
Stage set and projections for *Magical Music*, a touring show in which the best known Disney tunes were performed by a symphony orchestra.

7
Launch event for the Broadgate development in London.

8
Presentation set for Ford Business TV.

9
Holiday Inn conference, Atlanta.

10
Ford stand at the Geneva Motor Show.

11
Environment created for the aftershow party of the musical *Copacabana*, hosted by the Imagination Gallery.

12
Exhibit from 'Megabugs', an exhibition on insects at the Natural History Museum.

13
Touring game show designed to promote the new EuroDisney theme park (now Disneyland Paris).

14
Studio set for the TV series 'Blind Date'.

15
Office interior for the International Wool Secretariat in Leeds.

16, 17
Plan and rendering of a proposed lighting scheme for Croydon town centre.

18
The Sandwich Box, a food outlet at the Aylesbury branch of supermarket Safeway, designed by Virgile & Stone.

19, 20
Pitch for the opening of the World Ski Championships in Sierra Nevada, Spain and concept model of a presentation stage.

Imagination Entertainments
While Imagination has always introduced elements
of theatre into its work, it was not until the late 1980s
that the company seriously began to engage with
pure entertainment, following a commission to design
elements of a stage set for the West End musical *Time*.
As its involvement grew, it began to contemplate
creating theatrical productions entirely on its own,
and in 1989 Imagination Entertainments was set up to
draw on Imagination's creative and technical resources
both for conventional theatrical productions and for
use in the company's communications activities.

1994

1, 2
Stage set concept for an Elton
John tour. The hydraulically
animated projection
screens would carry imagery
relevant to each of the songs
performed.

3
London Weekend Television's
live Christmas broadcast
from Imagination's offices,
featuring highlights
from West End musicals
including Barry Manilow's
Copacabana for which
Imagination designed the set
and projections.

4, 5
Model showing proposed
redevelopment of London's
Battersea Power Station
as an entertainment-led retail
and leisure destination, for
Parkview International.

6, 7
Spreads from Ford's *Car
Driver's Guide*.

8
Ford stand at the Birmingham
Motor Show.

9
Concept model for a BT
exhibition.

10
Multimedia display for a
BT exhibition stand at Geneva
Telecom.

11, 12
St Paul's Cathedral illuminated
for *The Music of Andrew Lloyd
Webber*, a gala performance
in aid of the Lord Mayor's
Appeal for St Paul's, produced
by Imagination Entertainments.

13
Stage set and projections for
The Risen People at the Gaiety
Theatre, Dublin, commissioned
by Playtime Productions and
Hell's Kitchen.

14
Exhibition stand for BT.

15
'The Fantasy Factory',
a visitor attraction for children
at Cadbury's chocolate-
production plant, Bourneville.

16
Stage set for the musical
Once on This Island at
London's Royalty Theatre.

17
Street-side hoarding promoting
the musical *Once on This Island*.
A family lived full-time for ten
days on a Caribbean beach on
the side of London's busy
Cromwell Road.

18
Plan showing proposal for a
branded Marlboro club.

19
Proposed re-use of the touring
Sleeping Beauty Castle
designed by Imagination for
Disney; the Castle is surrounded
by cherry picker cranes holding
up a 360-degree fabric loop,
on which projections can
be viewed from both inside
and outside the loop.

20
Design of all public spaces
including reception and
meeting rooms for the London
offices of financial public
relations consultancy Dewe
Rogerson, by Virgile & Stone.

21
Website for BT.

22 23, 24, 25
Stills from a film created for
the Pharmacia privatization
roadshow.

26
Entertainments organized in
conjunction with Disney for
a gala dinner at a Holiday Inn
conference in Orlando, Florida.

27
Pilot episode of a TV version
of the radio programme
'The Moral Maze', filmed in the
Imagination Building.

1995

1
Exhibition in the Imagination Gallery to mark the publication of *Experience*.

2
Concept model for a touring Lego brand experience.

3
Concept model of 'Earthquest', an installation for the Earth Galleries at London's Natural History Museum.

4
Environment for Ford's Business Meeting in Birmingham.

5, 6
Spreads from a brochure designed to promote the Ford Galaxy.

7
Presentation for the National Westminster Bank.

8
Brochure for the NEC in Birmingham.

9
Print advertising campaign for the Royal Mail.

10
Lighting scheme for insurance company Prudential.

11
Early version of Imagination's own website.

12
Animated typography for British Army TV advertising campaign, through Saatchi & Saatchi.

13
Concept model of a touring brand centre, originally designed for Coca-Cola.

14
Concept model of Adventure One, a touring brand centre.

15
BT exhibition stand at CeBIT '95.

16
Illumination on the face of the Imagination Building to mark the opening night of the musical *Tutankhamun*.

17
Exhibition stand for Ford's Automotive Components Division at Frankfurt Motor Show.

18
Exhibition stand for BT at Telcom '95 in Geneva.

19
Corporate brochure for Andersen Consulting.

20
Mezzanine, a restaurant in the Royal National Theatre, London, designed by Virgile & Stone.

21
Invitation to the launch of Work, a new range of furniture by Intercraft.

22
Proposal for a scheme using projections, multimedia and lighting on site hoardings as part of a communications strategy during BAA's redevelopment of Heathrow Airport.

23
Concept model showing environment for Iveco Ford's 20th anniversary event.

24
BT's 'Livetalk' exhibition stand at Olympia, London.

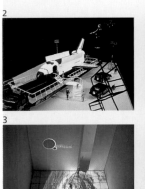

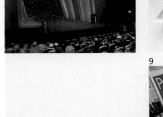
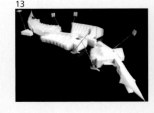

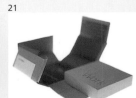

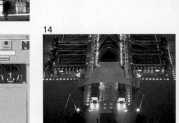

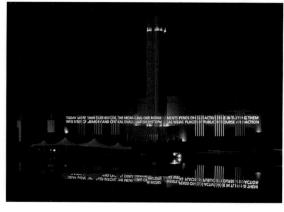

25, 26
Concept models showing proposed illuminations, to alert the public to the fact that Bankside Power Station was being converted into the Tate Modern art gallery.

27
Live performance on BT's 'Livetalk' exhibition stand.

28, 29
Merchandise for Cadbury's 'Fantasy Factory' visitor attraction.

30
Illuminations and firework display centred on BT's Telecom Tower to mark the 50th anniversary of VE Day.

31
Virtual Reality display on the Ford stand at Frankfurt Motor Show.

32, 33
Poster advertising campaign for the Prince's Trust, a youth charity.

34
Promotional film for the Ford Galaxy.

35
Ford 'Fleet News' show at Silverstone race track.

36
Concept model of Ford's Edgware Road car dealership for which Imagination designed the interior.

37
Concept model of the Utopia Pavilion at the Lisbon Expo.

38
Concept renderings of The National Explorium Centre, a proposed visitor attraction commissioned by Plymouth Development Corporation.

39
Graphic display from the Ford stand at the Frankfurt Motor Show.

40
Ford stand at the London Motor Show.

41
Virgin Beach, a proposal for a Virgin holiday destination.

42, 43, 44, 45
Illuminated interactive walkways and exhibits on Ford's stand at the Barcelona Motor Show.

46, 47, 48
Stills from *BT Business Solutions*, one of a series of four films made for the telecoms company.

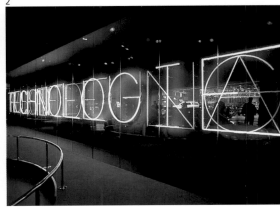

1996

1, 2
Neon display from Ford's stand at the Geneva Motor Show.

3, 4, 5
Display on safety comprising graphics, film, lighting and projections from Ford's stand at the Brussels Motor Show.

6
Town lighting scheme for Weymouth, Dorset.

7, 8, 9
Cover and spreads from BT's *TalkWorks* booklet, which discussed ways to improve interpersonal communications.

10, 11
Exhibits from Ford Automotive Components Division's stand at the Birmingham Motor Show.

12
Christmas tree in Imagination's atrium.

13
Interior and exterior lighting scheme for the cruise ship, *Disney Magic*.

14
Structure designed to house the reveal of the Ford Mondeo.

15
Display from the Ford stand at the Ulster Motor Show.

16
Stage set for the privatization roadshow of Pharmacia & Upjohn.

17
Concepts for an Ericsson visitor centre.

18
Ericsson exhibition stand at CeBIT '96 with live performers.

19
Still from Ericsson's *Performance* film.

20, 21
The London restaurant Mezzo was converted into the Ka Café for a day to launch the Ford Ka.

Virgile & Stone
The architecture and interior design consultancy Virgile & Stone is a wholly owned subsidiary of Imagination. Its two partners, Carlos Virgile and Nigel Stone approached Gary Withers in 1990 with a view to setting up their own company under the Imagination umbrella. The new company brought in a different type of client and project, which have ranged from interiors for night clubs in the Far East to restaurant chains and department stores.

22
Homewares and furniture store Heal's in the King's Road, London, designed by Virgile & Stone.

23
The Wheelie Toy, a children's toy made from recycled plastic bottles. Developed by Imagination from an original concept by its inventor.

24
Stage set and environment for Ford's quarterly Business Meeting.

25, 26, 27
Presentation document for the pitch to design the environment for the Atlanta Olympics.

28, 29, 30
Lego Driving School at LegoLand in Windsor.

31, 32
CD-ROM and brochure designed for Ford's stand at the Paris Motor Show.

33
Ford 'Fleet News' show.

34
Ford stand at the Ulster Motor Show.

35
Stage set for Deutsche Telekom's privatization roadshow.

36
Stage set for Argentaria's privatization roadshow.

37
Stage set for British Energy's privatization roadshow.

38
Director Isaac Mizrahi at the premiere party for his film *Unzipped*, held at the Imagination Gallery.

39, 40, 41
Stills from a brand film for the Ford Ka.

42
Concept model showing 'Islands of Adventure', a proposed attraction for Universal Studios.

43, 44
The launch of a range of Thompson televisions designed by Phillipe Starck, held in the Imagination Gallery.

1997

1, 2
Concept work for Millennium Central; the rendering shows 'No Time to Waste', a proposed exhibit on recycling.

3, 4
Studio set for the TV sports chat show 'On Side'.

5
Concept model showing interior of Capital Ford, a car dealership in London's Edgware Road.

6
Ford stand at Frankfurt Motor Show.

7
Literature for the Eden Project, a biospheres network in Cornwall.

8, 9
Ford stand at the Geneva Motor Show.

10
Exhibition stand for Electrolux.

11
Ericsson conference environment.

12
Literature for Ericsson 'IFA' conference.

13
Chez Gérard restaurant in Bishopsgate, London, designed by Virgile & Stone.

14
Ericsson Voice stand at CeBIT '97.

15, 16
Two Zero Two, a nightclub in Samsung's Hotel Shilla in Seoul, Korea, designed by Virgile & Stone.

17, 18
Film for Canada's CN Rail AGM.

19, 20, 21
Displays from Ford's stand at the Barcelona Motor Show.

22, 23, 24
Concept models of the Guinness Storehouse.

25
Dark ride at the Cadbury 'Fantasy Factory' in Bourneville, UK.

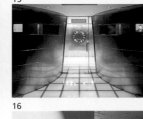

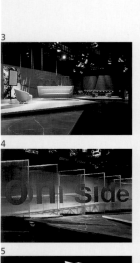

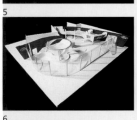

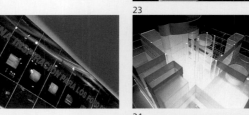
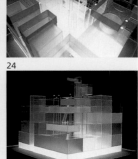

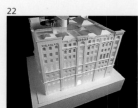

The Imagination Gallery
The 200 sq m (2,150 sq ft) space under the fabric canopy at the top of the Imagination Building was originally intended to be the company's presentation suite, but was quickly repurposed as the Imagination Gallery. Since 1990, the Imagination Gallery has hosted around 200 events a year ranging from product launches to fashion shows, banquets to award ceremonies, in the process becoming one of London's best known venues.

26

26
Trapeze artists performed at the launch of hairdresser Charles Worthington's Impact range of products at The Imagination Gallery.

27, 28, 29
Paris Motor Show stand and literature for Visteon, an automotive components manufacturer.

30
CD-ROM designed for Ericsson's Voice stand at CeBIT '97.

31
ericsson.bond.com, a website designed to promote Ericsson's sponsorship of the Bond film *Tomorrow Never Dies*.

32
Concept model of the new Central Lounge at Amsterdam Airport Schiphol, designed by Virgile & Stone.

33, 37
Brochure and carrier bag for Ericsson's Voice stand at CeBIT '97.

34
Lego Toyfair exhibition stand.

35, 36
Ericsson's stand and literature for a Berlin trade show.

38
Brand guidelines for Ericsson's research and development departments.

39, 40, 41, 42, 43
Interactive multimedia walkway on the Ford stand at the Barcelona Motor Show.

44
Concept design work for the fascia of a Ford car dealership in Amsterdam.

45
Lighting scheme for the Oracle department store in Reading.

46, 47
Cover and spread from the book *This is Your Brand*, designed for Ericsson employees.

48
Postcards designed to mark the launch of the Ford Puma at the Geneva Motor Show.

49
Ericsson conference environment.

50, 51
Julien Macdonald fashion show in the Imagination Gallery, with photographs by Sean Ellis.

199

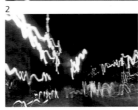

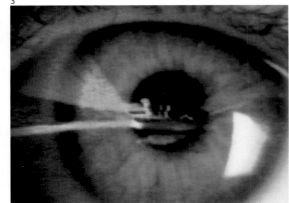

1998

1, 2, 3
Stills from a film depicting the increasing pace of modern life, created for the Aurora Centre in Berlin.

4
The Ford stand at the Geneva Motor Show.

5
'Teaser' site promoting the new Imagination website.

6, 7
Lego Toyfair exhibition stand.

8, 9, 10
Literature, film component and facade of the Aurora Centre, the temporary home of the Ford brand designed to house a seven-week event for Ford dealers in Berlin.

11
The Virtual Shop, an interactive multimedia presentation designed to allow dealers visiting Ericsson's stand at CeBIT '98 to configure their own retail outlets.

12
Yves Saint Laurent shop in Paris, designed by Virgile & Stone.

13
Press event announcing BT's sponsorship of a zone in the Millennium Dome. Projections told the story on the fabric roof of the Dome.

14
Exhibition in The Imagination Gallery on TalkWorks, a BT initiative designed to help people improve their communication skills.

15, 16
Signage and literature for Ericsson's 'GSM Summit' conference in Stockholm.

17, 18, 19
Ericsson's exhibition stand at CeBIT '98, whose design was based on its then current advertising strapline, 'Make yourself heard'.

20, 21, 22
New corporate identity designed for the National Exhibition Centre and associated enterprises in Birmingham.

23
The Ford stand at the Birmingham Motor Show.

24, 25, 26
Stills from the film *Make Yourself Heard*, shown on Ericsson's stand at CeBIT '98, in which people from around the world expressed their hopes, wishes, dreams and beliefs.

Journey Ford
— 1

talk
— 3

skyscape
— 5

2

4

6

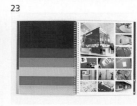

1999

1, 2
Logotype and architecture of Journey, the pavilion in the Millennium Dome dedicated to transportation.

3, 4
Logotype and architecture of Talk, the communication pavilion in the Millennium Dome.

5, 6
Logotype and entertainment installation for Skyscape, the cinema at the Millennium Dome, sponsored by Sky.

7, 8
Ford Motor Company's Trustmark stand at the North American International Auto Show in Detroit.

9
The Spice Girls launch their book, *Spice Girls,* in the Imagination Gallery.

10, 11
Environment for '+connect', an event for North American Ford dealers held in Philadelphia.

12
Registration website for Ericsson's 'Fast Thinking, Fast Future' conference, held in California.

13
One of a set of postcards designed for Ericsson's stand at CeBIT '98.

14
Futureforests.com, a website designed for environmental task force Future Forests.

15
Millennium display area on Ford's stand at the London Motor Show.

16
Identity and CD packaging for Sound Space, an educational initiative organized by London Open House, directed at young people with an interest in architecture.

17
Environment for Ericsson's wwwireless ambition conference, designed and organized by Imagination.

18
Ericsson's stand at Telecom '99 in Geneva.

19, 20
Ericsson mobile phone packaging and product packaging guidelines, produced by Imagination to ensure consistency across Ericsson's entire range of products around the world.

21
Demountable exhibition stand designed for watchmaker Patek Philippe by Virgile & Stone.

22, 23
Slip case and spread from the *Ericsson Events Guidelines,* produced to ensure consistency across all of Ericsson's face-to-face communications activities around the world.

24, 25
Now Generation exhibition stand and photography detail for Ericsson at CeBIT '98.

26
Packaging prototypes for a new range of cosmetics, commissioned by Unilever.

27, 28
CD-ROM on Ford's 021C concept car, in packaging designed by Marc Newson.

29, 30
Frankfurt Motor Show exhibition stand and literature for Visteon, an automotive components manufacturer.

31, 32, 33
Stills sequence from one of eight films created for Ford Motor Company's Trustmark stand at the North American International Auto Show. This film, on the type of people who work for Ford, focused on a Ford employee and part-time volunteer fire-fighter.

7

12

17

22

27

8
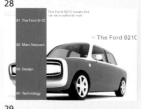

13

18
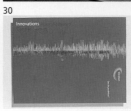

23
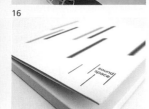

28

31

9

14

19

24

29
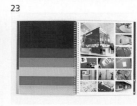

32

10

15

20

25

30

33

11

16
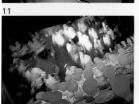

21

26

Imagination USA Inc.
Imagination has maintained a presence in the USA since 1988, when it first tested the water with a small New York office. A further outpost in Atlanta followed, but it was not until 1999 that the company set up its first entirely autonomous, American office, with its own full complement of creative, technical and production management staff. Trading as Imagination (USA) Inc., the company moved into its current premises in TriBeCa, New York City and Detroit, Michigan, the following year.

2000

1, 2
Environment for '+connect', an event for North American Ford dealers held in Atlanta.

3
Website for the Guinness Storehouse.

4, 5, 6
Interior views of the Guinness Storehouse.

7
Lighting design scheme for Regent Street, London.

8, 9
Environment for Barclays 'eday', an event designed to communicate the bank's digital strategy to analysts and the media.

10, 11
Environment and literature for 'Open', a touring series of face-to-face meetings between the new chief executive of Barclays and the bank's staff around the world.

12
Website designed to carry the message of Barclays' 'eday' event to a wider public.

13, 14
Environment and display for Ford's stand at the Birmingham Motor Show.

15, 19
Environment for Ericsson's 'Making Sense of the New Economy' conference.

16
Exhibition at London's Design Museum of the work of designer Marc Newson.

17, 18
Exhibition stand for Visteon at the Paris Motor Show.

20
Concept proposals for a Ford Mustang retail brand experience.

21, 22
Exhibition stand and multimedia display for Ericsson at CeBIT 2000.

23, 24
Environment for the Coca-Cola Lifehouse, an event for the senior staff of the Coca-Cola Company, held in Berlin.

25, 26
Technical exhibits on Ford's stand at the Birmingham Motor Show.

27, 28
Invitation and environment for Ericsson's 'Fast Thinking, Fast Future' conference, held in California.

29

30

31

29, 30, 31
Ford's stand at the Birmingham Motor Show.

32
The Collection shop at VW Autostadt, Wolfsburg, Germany, designed by Virgile & Stone.

33, 34
Graphic language developed for an event held over several weeks in Seville, Spain, in which Ford dealers were able to drive and appraise the new Ford Transit.

35
Lighting design scheme for a telecoms mast owned by the mobile phone operator Orange.

36
Proposal for HSBC branding in the boarding tunnels at Heathrow Airport.

37, 38
Environment and postcard for the launch of the new Ford Mondeo, held on Ford's stand at the Paris Motor Show.

39
Exterior signage for an Ericsson conference in Monte Carlo.

40
Still from *Telematics*, an animated multimedia presentation on new in-car communications technologies, designed for Ford's stand at the Geneva Motor Show.

41, 42, 43
Stills from a brand film for the Ford Galaxy.

44
Proposal for a website to tie in with a Volvo product launch.

45
Exhibition stand for wireless Internet operating system developer Symbian at CeBIT 2000. The 'departures' theme reflected Symbian's desire for partners on its journey into the technological future.

46, 47
Cover and spread from *Journey*, a book produced by Imagination to document its work on the Millennium Dome pavilion.

48
Identity for Exos, a proposed environment in which Ford staff could immerse themselves in contemporary cultural trends.

49, 50
Model and exterior rendering of Ford College, a dealer training school attached to Loughborough University.

51, 52
Cover and spread from *talk*, a book produced by Imagination to document its work on the Millennium Dome pavilion.

53, 55
'BT Openworld', an event designed to launch BT's broadband Internet services, held in the Imagination Building.

54
Visitor centre at Ericsson's corporate headquarters in Kista, Sweden.

32

36

41

46

51

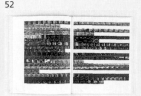
54

33

37

42

47

52

34

38

43

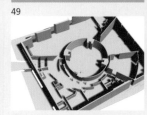
48

53

55

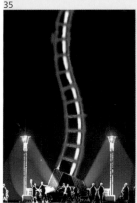
35

39

44

49

40

45

50

Index

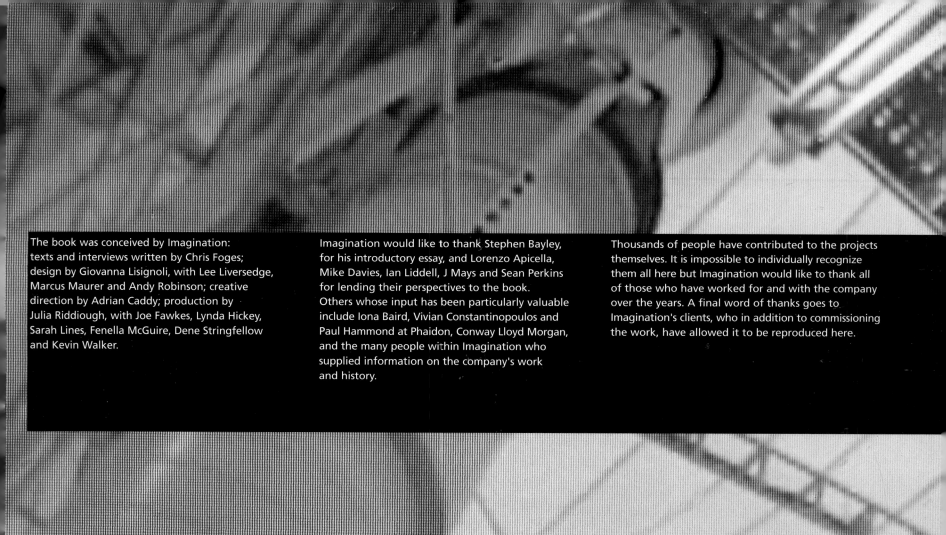

The book was conceived by Imagination: texts and interviews written by Chris Foges; design by Giovanna Lisignoli, with Lee Liversedge, Marcus Maurer and Andy Robinson; creative direction by Adrian Caddy; production by Julia Riddiough, with Joe Fawkes, Lynda Hickey, Sarah Lines, Fenella McGuire, Dene Stringfellow and Kevin Walker.

Imagination would like to thank Stephen Bayley, for his introductory essay, and Lorenzo Apicella, Mike Davies, Ian Liddell, J Mays and Sean Perkins for lending their perspectives to the book. Others whose input has been particularly valuable include Iona Baird, Vivian Constantinopoulos and Paul Hammond at Phaidon, Conway Lloyd Morgan, and the many people within Imagination who supplied information on the company's work and history.

Thousands of people have contributed to the projects themselves. It is impossible to individually recognize them all here but Imagination would like to thank all of those who have worked for and with the company over the years. A final word of thanks goes to Imagination's clients, who in addition to commissioning the work, have allowed it to be reproduced here.